# AIMING

# FOR

# BALANCE

The Power of COS VAP in
Structured Thinking

## James Noll

C.O.S = COMPONENTS, ORDER, STEPS
V.A.P = VIEWPOINT, ATTENTION, PERCEPTION

Aiming for Balance

The Power of COS VAP in Structured Thinking

©2025, James Noll

All rights reserved. This book or any portion thereof may not be reproduced or used in any manner whatsoever without the express written permission of the publisher except for the use of brief quotations in a book review.

ISBN: 979-8-35099-290-8

ISBN eBook: 979-8-35099-291-5

For Dave,

If this succeeds I'll revel in the glory. If it fails I'm blaming you for the idea!

James Noll

# TABLE OF CONTENTS

1. Introduction ................................................................. 1
2. Point(s) of Order ....................................................... 11
3. The Necessity of Aim ............................................... 19
4. Vision ........................................................................ 27
5. Viewpoint .................................................................. 31
6. Attention ................................................................... 37
7. Perception ................................................................. 45
8. Narrative and Linguistic Aspects of Perception .......... 47
9. The Role of Perception in Decision Making ............... 63
10. Works Cited .............................................................. 73

"In the following pages I offer nothing more than simple facts, plain arguments, and common sense; and have no other preliminaries to settle with the reader, than that he will divest himself of prejudice and prepossession, and suffer his reason and his feelings to determine for themselves; that he will put on, or rather that he will not put off, the true character of a man, and generously enlarge his views beyond the present day."

*— Thomas Paine*

# INTRODUCTION

Throughout my life, I've contended with ideas, experiences, interpretations, and people. I suspect I'm not alone in this condition. The reader has and will undoubtedly encounter the many ways that life—good and bad, hard and easy, light and heavy—presents itself. These myriad of interpreted experiences are collected into frameworks within the mind, sequenced into behavior, and given a positive or negative association. When a past experience is replicated, or when one that is determined to be close enough occurs, we resurrect the relevant sequences of behavior and their attached values to process the new input. Consider tying your shoes. This action is a sequenced behavior built into a mental framework, associated with the positive or negative feelings of success or failure. Now that you're practiced at tying your shoes, the act is an automatic process, a pattern of thought married to behavior. This is part of Jean Piaget's four stages of cognitive development, which are the foundation for the processes that are implicit in this text.[1] Another way to think of the mental frameworks are like children's building blocks, with their shaded colors representing the feelings associated with a particular section, which has to fit with both the piece that precedes it and the one that follows. Frameworks like these, scaffolding built from simple concepts

---

[1] Jean Piaget and Barbel Inhelder, *The Psychology Of The Child,* trans. Helen Weaver (Basic Books, 1969).

with increasing complexity as they develop, often remain hidden within our day-to-day thought processes and are easily overlooked.

Our interpretations of experiences continuously alter or reinforce the hidden frameworks we use to think, speak, and act, affecting all aspects of our lives. These frameworks nest together in order to form a coherent narrative, using belief as a binder or ligament of sorts to smooth the edges of missing information or mal-formed narratives. The following writings explore how frameworks are supported by language, altered by individual and cultural forces, and are predicated on biological adaptation over countless generations. Although not inherently obvious, we can use the ideas I'm going to present to direct these frameworks and consequently bring immense benefits to our daily lives. The place to start any investigation or adventure is always by learning about the beginning, which, like these frameworks, should be consistently revisited.

A first consideration is that these valued frameworks take on a life of their own, functioning like their own sub-personality because they are rooted in our biological processes. An example of this is the instinctual function of fear that exists in all animals until they explore. As Jordan Peterson notes in *Maps of Meaning*, "Fear is not conditioned, security is unlearned."[2] Exploring leads to knowledge, which minimizes fear of the unknown; fear being the nascent state, while security exists because of our implicit assumptions that we are safe, until a new threat arises and we eventually learn to not be afraid of it.

This process of learning security in spite of the profound quantity of things we cannot know is a paramount aspect of the human experience. This procedure involves the interaction of our experiences woven with our biological responses into our linguistic representations, and then represented in both the stories we tell ourselves and those that have been culturally perpetuated. To expand what is happening, consider that within the developmental concepts of Piaget are three categories of connected ideas: the first of these is action, imitation, and play. The key to this grouping is imitation, in part because despite its necessity to our early development, imitation will always remain one of the most powerful tools in our mental toolbox. This

---

[2] Jordan B. Peterson, *Maps of Meaning: The Architecture of Belief* (Routledge, 1999), 57.

crucial piece of hardware in the human mental computer—imitation—is what initially facilitates our development from basic functions to understanding symbols. Symbols form words, which in turn form language, and language is the key to the second group: ritual, drama, and narrative. As our operations become more concrete, individual narratives interacting with other narratives eventually form the final group: myth, religion, philosophy, and rationalization. The interpretation of abstractions at this level of development depends solely on how we rationalize them and, by extension, how we evaluate categories of connected concepts.

Categories of connected concepts like existential danger and redeeming hope, evil and good, or negative and positive are just a few of these linguistic adaptations to the human condition that are woven into our frameworks. I put the categories in a different order than how they are usually spoken because even small changes in language will have large effects on how we rationalize. Ask yourself, *If language isn't tied to human function, why would we always say good versus evil, and not the other way around?* If reading my mis-ordering makes you feel something without thinking about it, then you have recognized one place where your biology, language, and human functionality have been married. Despite living in general comfort and safety, these developmental processes have mixed with our biological responses, like the fear of the unknown. This is the same fear that our ancestors experienced, whether it is the fear of losing a job or the fear when you realize a panther has been stalking you.

Due to the primal nature of the fear response, it's a crucial place to investigate the role our mental frameworks play in shaping our thoughts and behaviors, and their impact on the world around us. Among the many reasons to be aware of this link is this important one: fear is a powerful motivator and as such becomes a weapon, intentional or not. Barry Glassner highlights numerous examples in his book, *Culture of Fear,* like the misplaced fear surrounding Halloween candy poisoning given that, at the time of his writing, "the only two known cases where children apparently did die from

Halloween candy, the myth of the anonymous sadistic stranger was used to cover up the real crime."[3]

Glassner's work shows that for decades there has been profound manipulation through fear, even when rational conclusions are easily available. Imagine someone who uses a drug like heroin willingly giving it to a random child, or a parent who misses the distinctly vacant shape left by an imbedded razor blade, or the indentation and discoloration that results from forcing anything into an apple. A well known but ignored fact of human nature that would dispel the fear is not considered; heroin addicts are not willingly giving away their heroin without something in return. Yet, every year this fear is revived and people become more suspicious of the stranger who willingly gives to their neighbors without an expectation of return. Fear of losing what we value most makes even the simplest scrutiny of knowledge secondary, at least until the fear subsides. This only amplifies in our modern lives, as the Internet exponentially exposes us to these psychologically maximized fear and propaganda purveyors. As our structured frameworks are exposed to information, carefully examined or not, they readily crystallize into beliefs and habits.

Let's take a habit that may not be serving you well, like an addiction to alcohol. This short-term positively reinforced behavior, if left unchecked, may result in long-term negative consequences. Each time we use a substance like alcohol, the positive value we place in our mental framework strengthens our behavior regarding alcohol use. The control this structure has over our behavior becomes harder to ignore, because the temporary good feeling reinforces the drinking behavior, thereby creating the habit. To counteract this framework, we must build a new, equally fortified framework. Starting small and gradually building a reformed behavioral response the same way the negative habit was built is crucial if we wish to change. This new set of behaviors should benefit us as a whole, rather than catering to the original patterns' short-sighted motivations. Ideas like the twelve-step program for alcoholism exemplify this process, which is rooted in religious thinking.

---

[3] Barry Glassner, *The Culture of Fear: Why Americans Are Afraid of the Wrong Things: Crime, Drugs, Minorities, Teen Moms, Killer Kids, Mutant Microbes, Plane Crashes, Road Rage, & So Much More* (Basic Books, 2009), 30.

The example of the twelve-step program illustrates the power of language in re-building sequenced behavior frameworks that guide our actions. The aim of this text is to help us recognize how pervasive these patterned sequences are, understand their historical and biological foundations, recognize when it's appropriate to adjust these value frameworks, and shape them to benefit our future selves. This motivation drives these writings, offering starting points for investigating these thought filters, referred to as Components, Order, and Steps (COS) and Viewpoint, Attention, and Perception (VAP). These categories may not represent all of the relevant information, and they may have overlap given the specific situation. Terms like filter, lens, structures, or patterns will be used to describe similar phenomena of nested value frameworks for reasons that will become evident. COS VAP is the adaptable lens I'm presenting as a starting point through which our cognitive structures may be expressed.

Many traditional religious texts, classical literature, and even modern movies highlight symbolic representation through narrative in an engaging, rewarding, surreal, and ultra-real way. Consider that with every word and image in a movie, as we sink deeper into an almost trance-like state, we absorb the experience as if we are there, while paradoxically remaining disembodied from the action, which can hinder solidifying these experiences into memory. This deep attraction to repeated narratives can be seen as versions of enduring human experiences transposed into verbally expressed values over time, reflecting Carl Jung's idea of archetypes. As Jung stated regarding his concept of the collective unconscious, "It's not about inherited ideas, it's about inherited patterns of thought."[4] This means we are not strictly handed ideas to believe, we are imbued with the frameworks of interpretation that lead us to similar conclusions and then representations.

These inherited patterns of thought are repeatedly echoed in stories, uniting people's interpretations of the world around them regardless of whether they had exactly the same experiences. Stories can be challenging to recall in full or to understand their deeper metaphors. Often, they evoke straightforward emotions, but occasionally they prompt deeper reflection.

---

[4] Carl Gustav Jung, *The Archetypes and the Collective Unconscious*, trans. Richard Francis Carrington Hull (Routledge, 1991), 3-12.

The parts of a story we find meaningful and hence remember depend on their relevance to our current life path and interests. Without the meaningful connection to our individual frameworks, it's very challenging to remain attentive and engaged.

When you come to resurrect past narratives, thoughts, or experiences, you likely weren't ready to accept all it had to give you at the time you were engaged with it. When taking the small steps to build your frameworks, you need the foundational structure to springboard from which our mentors and their stories contain. Many other things obscure careful thinking, like current events, problems in your life, or things you'd like to accomplish. The distractions pop up like a new window on a bad website, hiding the moving parts that guide our thinking. Scientifically, this concept of knowledge resting just below the next achievable step is supported by Vgotsky's Zone of Proximal development, which emphasizes starting from the edge of what you know to best facilitate learning.[5] You may have heard a parent or mentor say something for decades and one day, when it becomes relevant, almost like an epiphany, you recognize where the mentor's words fit in your current understanding. This knowledge allows us to aim accurately at the next step, but only if we know what step we are on. My aim is to establish the concepts of COS VAP in a way that is close to your developmental position as well as making them practical and applicable for everyday use.

This brings us to an important consideration. Narratives are representations about what we value most and how to act according to those values. As we act, imitate, and play, we are automatically building individual hierarchies of value because we inherently elevate some conceptions or circumstances over others. What we deem the most highly valued may be conceived of what we personally believe to be divine. After many generations, myths, religion, and philosophies codify the values into texts, like the Bible as the word of God. The consequence is that characters develop the same way, becoming archetypal—such as the highest-valued human—by representing themes such as hero and anti-hero, order and chaos, good and evil, black and white, stasis and change, to name a few.

---

[5] Charles Fernyhough and Peter Lloyd, ed, *Lev Vygotsky: Critical Assessments* (Routledge, 1999), 259-279.

We are hardwired to interpret these characteristics—even within complex narratives, as well as their interactions with other individuals, institutions, cultures, or opposing ideas—through metaphor. When engaged with a narrative, we can't help but make direct comparisons of ourselves to the characters or groups, allowing for the easiest uptake of these behaviors and ideas. Other times, more complex metaphors are buried within the interactions of characters we have an instinctual distaste for, such as the anti-hero, hardly pausing to listen as our inherent mental structures guide our interpretations. Metaphor is fundamental to our conceptual systems by framing concepts through embodied experiences.[6]

There are many instances where our modern sensibilities about morality clash with past stories and their recommendations. We should be cautious in discerning what is good and bad, acknowledging that neither you nor I alone can definitively judge what is good and what is bad, if only because you must have more than one human for morality to matter at all. We must collect and disseminate widely accepted morality and unifying codes of ethics if we are to operate effectively as the social creatures that we naturally are.

I will sometimes try to highlight interpretations of individual words to reveal meanings that might otherwise be overlooked. For example, *information* seeks to inform formation. Words, like structures, have undergone construction over time; humanity has used language to build up values into something akin to a locked safe, secure and very resistant to change, similar to structures within a home. This locked-safe metaphor is one of many linked to the structures of the mind, sturdy and therefore difficult to change easily.[7] The term *understand* is that which is under you that allows you to stand. Character is both an identity that is acted out and an expression of a universally accepted ethic. Carefully understanding the meaning of words allows us to see that understanding is the foundation of all narratives, an easily overlooked aspect of profound significance. These links, words, metaphor, narrative are among the strands that weave together to produce the thought filters we will be discussing: COS, as well as VAP. This framework will help us

---

[6] George Lakoff and Mark Johnson, *Metaphors we live by* (University of Chicago Press, 2003), 3-15.

[7] Lakoff and Johnson, *Metaphors we live by*, 15-32.

discern, organize, and align our thoughts and actions in a way that supports both personal and collective growth.

Some strands will be characterized with words, like thought filter or lens, which are not exactly synonyms but different ways of seeing a similar concept, intended to help each reader find their preferred way of retaining the concepts. For example, *lens* connects to vision, which may be shaded like sunglasses. A *filter* sifts through in order to discern what to keep, like sunglasses shade the light of the sun. A framework suggests structure; much like the carbon of a water filter, the structure is what makes it effective.

If it is reasonable to suggest that part of the foundation of civilization is expressed through short statements or stories intended to guide individual behavior—something propaganda is designed to exploit—then when individuals of various backgrounds and their ethics, narratives, and values integrate into large-scale human collaboration, it becomes clear that too much ethical variance disrupts cohesion. Therefore, as narratives distill behavioral information into simple, actionable guidance, they enable individuals to function harmoniously with one another when the metaphors of the narratives form ethics. This unity through mutual ethics implies a responsibility to yourself and others to carefully align your thoughts and values, understand how those thoughts influence your actions, and recognize how those actions impact both you and society. Metaphorically, this idea is the development of a child into an adult, a fertilized egg into a child, tracing back to the protozoa that led to all life. Everything that is built, just like society, has a structure, and all structures are built from the ground up.

If you agree with the power of the aforementioned concepts, you may also see that modern interactions often reflect opposing narratives within dogmatic dualities, such as group versus group. Being rigid in our beliefs leaves no room for the nuance within each individual, experience, or system. This dogmatism is evident when people repeat talking points that dismiss or deflect ideas that their value structure rejects. The simpler the nested value hierarchy is through which information is processed, the easier and more likely it is to be reinforced, often aiming to align the listener of the talking points with preconceived notions. This may lead to dismissing someone's entire character, identities, and beliefs based on one aspect of their values.

Assuming simplicity is accurate enough is akin to assuming that what you can't see doesn't exist.

    I am no less guilty of this bias of intention, especially in what I write. My intention is to emphasize the need for everyone to examine their thought structures and to provide some guides for doing that. I'm just as fallible as anyone else, and am trying to figure out how to operate best in the world using the information I've gathered. Perhaps something here can help you do the same.

    Many of the ideas I share were generated from others' brilliant minds, and I lay no claim to them. I'm fortunate to be able to be in their playground. I aim, by resting on those minds, to support a functional metric for evaluating our nested value structures, COS VAP. I seek to transcend the human tendency toward selfish interest, such as bringing the reader into my formation, and aim to reconnect you to the wisdom of the past that informs the future.

    I do not claim that the information I present is all-inclusive or entirely original. I am merely collecting what I think may be helpful if considered first and applied to circumstances and ideas to minimize misdirection. The title of these writings conveys the necessity of balance in human life and indicates that every idea I present comes with a competing angle. An alternate hypothesis may apply given the appropriate circumstances, and my omissions are not meant to suggest otherwise.

# POINT(S) OF ORDER

That which sticks, that which is identifiable, that which establishes, that which marks, that which pierces, that which matters, may be regarded as a point. Humans have created linguistic adaptations such as "get to the point" or "at what point," which are taking the abstraction power of the brain and linking it to objects in the world so that the combined wisdom may be shared with others. These points are the root of cooperative civilization that benefits from the gathering of information from an individual that is then made available to the many.

The significance of points is the distillation down to what matters, and matter is, like points, another great linguistic linkage that represents both what things are made of and what is important. Matter is the maternal, that which brings all life, and metaphorically is the root of all possibility. Links like these are the fundamental building blocks of our complex interpretive structures, through abstract representations that are scaffolded from the bottom up and then again, boiling down the complex ideas into bite-size chunks of profound meaning. This refinement creates an increasingly sharp point, regardless of whether the point is made of metal or thought alone.

That which carries the point of an arrow and the energy behind it is the shaft, which begins the metaphor of archery that will permeate these writings. Archery is just one of the many ways these concepts of COS VAP can be applied to increase functionality. If we assume that a fundamental nature of humans is to recognize patterns, it stands to reason that when a human repeatedly recognized important patterns he would elevate and disseminate them. After many years of emergence, a pattern may be articulated into verbal expressions capable of—when harnessed properly—producing consistent results for someone thousands of years later. Such things underlie the basis of all stories and, in turn, if we already know the exact story or its lesson, we are less likely to engage with it unless it's presented in a new way.

In pursuit of such patterns, after attaching a sharp point to a shaft for example, it became obvious to the primordial man that his arrow wasn't quite working as he'd like it to work. Something else needed to be added, something gleaned from the muse, from the mysterious place which thought arises, from the ingenuity of man. When recognizing a pattern in nature—in this case that flying creatures had specific components like feathers—it became apparent that some of those components may prove useful to the balance necessary to right the flight of an arrow shaft. This became another component to the pattern of recognizing how man can adapt nature to his benefit and was integrated into our language and stories.

This recognition is the undeniable aspect of human nature that interacts with the world. Such functionality requires steps—that which physically moves you forward—and components necessary to functionality and order—how to orient the steps or components. COS are most often only applied to a given situation; meaning the steps and order may need to change given the circumstances, but some aspects of COS will remain constant. Throughout this text, the COS will present themselves, as will the need to recognize VAP, which will be covered in more detail later.

Let's assume that we can't know everything, and therefore the COS of a given situation isn't clearly visible without significant prior investigation and practice, as if you've never shot a traditional bow, like a recurve. We inherently accept that limitation when we are bringing abstract thoughts into being to interact with the world; we understand that there needs to be room to fill in the gaps in knowledge. A given COS is more than simply a belief we generally hold to be self-evident; COS is human functionality itself and may easily be ignored when forming a pattern that influences a person's actions. This represents a major challenge in the interplay between manipulating thoughts and objects to achieve the result we desire, as well as where I think this proverbial rubber meets the road.

If I had given different steps in the analogy of the components and order of an arrow, you could have made it to the end result of having an arrow eventually, but not quite as clearly or easily as when it was presented in a linear fashion. A discerning archer would note that I left out a nock, the term for where the arrow rests against a string, among a vast amount of other information necessary to make an arrow. A nock is just one missing component that, even if I had given you all the other pertinent information, causes failure.

This is an example of one small failure that can occur when you believe without investigation. Another might be if you assume an ingredient for dinner is in your cupboard but is not, or if while preparing spaghetti, you skip the step of boiling water for the pasta. If you ignore your responsibility to investigate your COS VAP, you ensure the possibility of functionality has a high likelihood of failure in your mind, before the idea even comes to interact with anything in the material world. Whether what you believe is because you already know or just willingly refuse to investigate doesn't matter. These types of thoughts are not birthing the possibility of new matter, as the maternal mother symbolically does.

Any idea someone presents you, myself included, doesn't become accurate simply because we have a feeling that it may be true, yet an idea needs feeling to be considered pursuit worthy. The idea only becomes accurate when you take the time to investigate the COS, bring the idea into the world by testing applicability, and repeat the experiment.[8] This is exactly what you are doing by reading this text. Sometimes we may be resistant due to a bias because of a negatively perceived belief, let's say Marxism. There may still be positive value to be found, like using questions to generate conflicting ideas—thesis against anti-thesis—resulting in synthesis, which was derived from Hegel, Marx's partner.[9] For our purposes, an idea that you bring into contact with the world meets a poignant question that illustrates fault in the conception; the result of forging a new idea is paramount to a sturdy founda-

---

[8] Herbert Alexander Simon, *Models of Thought* (Yale University Press, 1979), 85-105.

[9] Georg Wilhelm Friedrich. Hegel, *Phenomenology of Spirit*, ed John Niemeyer Findlay, trans Arnold V. Miller (Oxford University Press, 1977), 1-32.

tion. Whether an update is possible depends on whether you are interested in forging a new conception at all.

An example of changing what you are thinking might be in public speaking, a situation that many people have an aversion to. One solution offered is the idea to imagine the audience naked, while another might be to just speak to one person at a time. The strategies are often subjectively useful, but the need to adjust VAP remains constant. I've felt awkward and unmoored in front of just one person who might be very impressive; their character created an indentation in my idea of what is above me. To counteract this, I adjust my viewpoint to their height by thinking of them as a teenager or child, placing them on a peer-to-peer level with myself.

Here lies the potential that produces function, which then expands capability into what may become consistent accuracy. Functionality has as much to do with what and how you are thinking, maybe even more so, as it does with what you are interacting with. Due to the inevitability of human interaction and our shared fate, examining these processes of your mind is your duty to not just yourself but to humanity itself.

Let's apply this line of thinking to the archery metaphor. If the order is altered and you try to put feathers on the point of an arrow and the point up against the string of your bow, it becomes clear that failure is going to occur, given that you possess the conceptual framework of what an arrow looks like, which most people do. Herein lies a common failure of over-simplifying within a modern world rife with complicated and, the tier above, complex systems.

Simply because you have the representation at hand of the arrow failure does not mean you can build an arrow or know everything about the bow that propels it. There are many more facets of the steps and order in which, when aligned properly, will present the cursory knowledge necessary, in line with the material world, to produce such a marvel of human capability as the bow and arrow.

As you read on, consider this fundamental aspect of components, steps, and order within your own thoughts. Every time you encounter a situation where your mind is wrestling with a problem, experience, or potential solution, this is a reliable way that nature will allow you to get to the end result in the most expedient, least laborious, and least painful way. Only through examining your thoughts, steps, and order first and then bringing the components to bear on what you manipulate in the world, fluidly alternating depending on what presents itself, will anyone align with the effective and the possible. The moment we present a solution that is not grounded in our encapsulating knowledge of how something functions, we assume that our simplistic conclusions are anything more than a lie about our own capability, authenticity, or limitations.

It may be said lying is not fashionable, if for no other reason than to fashion—to assemble—based on a lie is a step toward failure, as well as what is in fashion—popular— will always be a truthful, capable, fair, and skilled person, given that society is not tyrannical. Lies are neither culturally acceptable nor will they allow for something of quality to be made from something false. Where character and skill are not held in the highest regard, lies and distrust will be found.

If we accept that language is only a step in communication, then we also accept that words are limited, if only in that we can't say all that needs to be said. In the last example, one could rightly clarify that the lie has to be seen as a lie for it to be culturally unacceptable. We should also consider that if we don't purposefully put limits on what we are saying, we aren't being accurate enough to express the truth as far as we know it. This belies the need to consistently establish what the words being used mean to each person speaking, as well as trying to determine why someone is speaking to them in the first place. Are they seeking to understand and be understood, or just to be understood? Does the person you are speaking with consider you a peer or a subordinate? Have they carefully considered the language they are using? If their speech is inaccurate, how can you be sure the error isn't intentional? Without mutual acceptance of what a word means, distrust and lies are soon to follow.

If the definitions of words have to be agreed upon, a statement is limited in what it describes, and the people talking are limited in what they can know, why don't we always assume these limitations when in a conversation? It would seem that this is among the foundational aspects of a functional conversation. We need to establish the point of why we are engaged in information sharing, as well as the components of how the conversation can be maximally optimized. If speaking to another person who does not enter into the conversation with an acceptance that there is more to know, has a good-faith basis, or is not treating you as a peer, it's not actually a conversation. Those circumstances are a chance for, among other things, that person to suggest their wisdom or superiority while unknowingly denying what we know to be true, we are all limited. Political debates are often an easy exemplar of this hubris.

If not tempered with the recognition of our own inadequacy, we denigrate the process of attaining knowledge itself. We are tempted to take shortcuts for a number of reasons, chief of which is brevity. This is where Carl Jung's statement, "beware unearned wisdom" begins to apply profound insights.[10] The expression implies the need to step from one zone of development to the next in repeated succession to attain wisdom. Jung suggests that without this progression, unearned wisdom has no authenticity, that is, it's not been self-authored and has not been carefully investigated. Those who strive to grapple with a particular subset of knowledge honestly and carefully, seeking to genuinely understand it, readily encounter how high the proverbial mountain of earned knowledge is. Since humility to such deep insight is the appropriate response, what does that say about those who are always certain of their wisdom?

When you stand in front of a mountain with the goal of reaching its summit, the profound nature of the experience clears the fog of simplicity along with any words that have been used to describe the task. The fear associated with the danger of traversing its broad and deep caverns, jagged and steep peaks,.corners and switchbacks hide the unknown. That profound feeling of humility is of the same quality that the seeker is forced to deal with when they are confronted by how little they can possibly know. This says nothing of all the other mountains of knowledge in the world. If you can't recognize this feeling you are missing the mountain in front of you.

Given that you are aware of these limitations, we turn to recognizing when the structure we use to interpret information may be overlooked.

---

[10] Carl G. Jung, *The Red Book: Liber Novus*, ed Sonu Shamdasani, trans Sonu Shamdasani (WW Norton, 2009), 35.

Ignoring both our limitations and what we are using to interpret the world is no different than ignoring the lightning storm while resting under the tallest tree. If you aren't carefully examining the way your mind is interpreting information, how each of us are prone to a given set of ideas and biases, as well as the fog that hides the aforementioned mountain of knowledge in a given domain, you are drastically reducing the chance of understanding: having that under you which allows you to stand.

This gap exposes the difference between a hack and a craftsman. A hack hopes someone doesn't look too closely at what they've produced, whereas a craftsman can be proud of their accomplishments because they have closely scrutinized the COS of their work. When having a bow and arrows built, you expect your trade of money and the time spent to attain it to support the point of your combined labors, something as valuable in return. Not examining our presuppositions and thought processes is the same as accepting your character is good enough, hoping other people may overlook the flaws. When the bow and arrows you receive are from a hack, you are instantly displeased with the lack of respect they gave to their craft and your investment in them.

If you recognize how poorly it feels to be on the receiving end of a hack job and if you compare the pride that comes from hard earned accomplishments, you may begin to see the benefit of what has been described surrounding the point of COS VAP. Ignoring COS or VAP ensures your endeavors are starting below 100 percent. To paraphrase something a wise man once told me, "If you convince yourself that 100 percent isn't worth striving for, if 80 percent is good enough, prepare to accept less than 80 percent." We are far too flawed to strive for anything less than 100 percent. Points, like the mind, need to be re-sharpened.

# THE NECESSITY OF AIM

Imagine yourself as an archer. If you try, you are repeating something many humans have done before you and, as a consequence, there are established ways of accomplishing the task. Maybe someone will suggest hunching your back over, angling the bow at 45 degrees, changing the orientation of your stance, or using a lower draw weight. A task such as this provides an almost instant link to past knowledge regarding orientation in the present and the possibility of aiding your pursuit of a promising future. The overall process requires meticulously and endlessly perfecting the archer's form so that the end result of hitting the mark occurs. Words from the past echo function into the future and are among the many advantages humans need to take seriously.

This process outlines a fundamental aspect that shooting a traditional bow echoes into everyone who tries to do it, as well as into their life broadly, highlighting an axiomatic belief that can be denied but at your peril. That axiom concerns ignoring your duty to know thyself, to work on your physical and mental form. Refusing to investigate the premises you hold will inevitably lead to dire consequences. You will make life for you and those around you worse than it already will be. In the archery example, the results could be as drastic as a glanced arrow that strikes someone else. If viewed through a rigid belief system, say a fundamentalist Christian sect, this could mean denying medical care that might be life-saving because the belief system requires the same thing as it did thousands of years ago. Deciding to forgo fixing the ignored or faulty elements of your relevant nested-value frameworks before you enter into an intimate relationship, for example, drastically increases the likelihood that you will fail, as well as the likelihood you will suffer miserably for it. You should ask yourself before such an endeavor, *How can I expect specific traits of another before I cultivate those same characteristics in myself?* If aim is necessary, why not aim for a better version of yourself?

If in the process of working on your form the appropriate order and steps of function do not occur, there has been an error, a sin, you are missing a key piece of information that would allow you to be in proper formation. Sin is more than just the religious term harkening eternal damnation in a metaphysical realm after you die. The biblical injunction can also be thought of in terms of the kind of hell you can create if you choose to repeatedly sin. On top of that sin is also a Greek archers term, *Hamartia*, meaning to miss the mark. Something as obviously out of order as aiming at your toe when you have drawn an arrow back strikes us as a foolish action, yet taking the overarching lesson of investigating COS remains unpracticed and disturbingly not echoed on a more uniform basis. The results are a sin in the religious sense of failing to be the most divine being as you can, codifying the sin of missing what you are aiming at in the material world.

Form in archery can be seen as an elevation of physical patterns that have shown the promise of success. Metaphorically speaking this crucial aspect that keeps us from sinning is about more than archery. If the premise of valued frameworks discussed in the preface are added to this conception of form, over time they lead to collective belief about how to effectively behave and eventually result in something approaching the social structure of morality, like that expressed in religious texts. Small changes in a personal approach to form, aligned with others who find similar concepts alluring that then unify over a shared belief system about how to perfect their form, elevates your combined aims toward the best version of what collective humanity could be. Moving upward, toward that which is above our current self—the celestial—is the point of aiming.

A crucial aspect of form in archery that plagues a shooter is keeping the bow hand solid through the shot. This is one aspect regarding the physical structure of form that can, if slightly off or unsteady at the point of release, undermine the basis of where a shot is going to end up. If you take the idea further, it underscores the nature of what connects life, standing tall in the face of your own suffering and limitations. This component of form is more than another step regarding archery; it's very hard to know what went wrong when shooting a bow as well as what went wrong in any failed endeavor, if for no other reason than the previously discussed profundity of knowledge can easily overwhelm our limited capacities. We need ways to cut through the fog of all possible failures to find what needs to change specifically, and investigating COS VAP provides the route.

Maybe, when thinking of your last shot, it wasn't the bow hand but the arm holding the bow that was slightly bent more than previous shots. Maybe the error was in resting the handle against the whole palm, as opposed to pinching with thumb and pointer finger only. Methodically unpacking what actions were performed, what story informed them, getting input from an outside observer on what they saw go wrong, and repeatedly trying are among the most effective ways to correct a sin. Without a structure to examine the story you are telling yourself, without examining your repeated sins, without others to point out failings that are invisible to you, hitting the mark enters into the realm of nearly impossible. As a boy I was able to play soccer, my then-focused pursuit, in Belgium for a tournament. The skill level of the competition was so disparate to my own that it shook the foundations of what I was aiming at, making an unopposable point about my previously unexamined beliefs. The framework I'd built through years of practice had foundational assumptions that, when I finally examined them, proved to be very de-stabilizing to the identity I'd created around my actions. These examinations of frameworks, and their relevant COS VAP, are among the things that help ground us in the face of seemingly infinite problems, facts, or ideas.

The difficulty comprehending the nature of what went wrong in an attempt at function requires speaking the truth as best you know it. When you encounter someone without the shared belief of at least not lying, discerning their motivations becomes of utmost importance and may be so profound it is paralyzing. This encounter renews the aforementioned unlearning of security, which results in resuming fear that is not conditioned. Becoming immobile, emotionally distraught, or stuck occurs not only because of the vast expanse of what there is to know about the dishonest person but is made more difficult because we are using the same system of comprehension with the same primordial brain functions that freezes a deer in headlights. Whether it's because of a demolished identity, liars, or a predator, our expanded thought capability is still bound by the biology of our evolutionary roots, compounding the effects of too much complexity.

Let's examine such an apparently simple statement as "build a house." The number of functional systems required to take the words and translate them into the result implied in the modern era stops nowhere near engineers, architects, design managers, contractors' secretaries, attendants at stores where materials are organized and purchased, factories in a foreign land thousands of miles away producing the materials for things such as faucets, or the people who actually put pre-assembled materials together on site. Add in the chance that some maligned human, striving to gain advantage outside the assumed rules of fair play our culturally shared belief finds acceptable, will lie, resulting in at least temporary failure to build the house.

The many moving parts that are steps in the complex action described within the simple statement *build a house* is why we rely on ancient stories, wisdom, repeatable results, trusted truth tellers, and cultural expectations like the fair play of other people. There really is no other option than to rely on other people, that we assume know what we don't know and are truthful, in such a circumstance. Yet the statement is so simple we can easily assume that which informs our COS or VAP are inconsequential. This is also why, along with limitations and the vast expanse of knowledge, you should, as Jordan Peterson admonished, "Assume the person you are listening to might know something you don't."[11]

When we are listening to someone, like a comedian for example, a crucial circumstance arises when trying to interpret the meaning of their words that may foster laughter. If the joke put forth follows a played-out premise, such as, "So and so walk into a bar," our constructs take us into the pattern of *bar* we've built up, which consists of things to be manipulated or interacted with in a bar such as drinks, glasses, pool tables, and so on. When

---

[11] Jordan B. Peterson, *12 Rules for Life: An Antidote to Chaos*, ed Norman Doidge (Random House Canada, 2018), 229.

the comedian mentions a stick, you're able to determine from your frameworks of *bar* that they probably mean pool stick, not a branch from a tree, bringing to mind the appropriate image. If you leave the relevant constructs by straying into other thoughts, once the joke progresses and you try to jump back in, you'll instantly notice a feeling of being lost. Unless you recognize the comedian's pattern of thought, you'll become an outsider searching for the entrance back in and will never find the joke funny.

In all the complexity of the world sits a human brain, which in itself is incredibly complicated. The brain is tasked with recognizing patterns, but also is in need of using those patterns constructed over time to simplify and categorize people and the world. Few things are more frightening or dangerous than being in a place where you can't recognize what someone may do next or what pattern would help avoid potential catastrophe. The accepted cultural rules of behavior or their snapshot indicators, such as "do you know so and so"—someone the questioner respects—ensures we can temporarily eliminate the complexity of other humans without the constant effort of re-evaluating what each new person with unknown behaviors may do at any moment. This temporary assumption of knowledge allows us to apply a framework that dismisses fear by coating the framework in belief and installing it as fully operational, leaving the assumed knowledge in place until the individual chooses to re-examine the thought structure.

Being that we are all limited in what we can know, we must accept some degree of framework assumption. This is among the most important updates necessary to achieve balance because we need mental and physical shortcuts to deal with our limitations, our values, and our desires. We must assign positive value to do anything, because otherwise we would do nothing, we can't know everything, we are prone to failure, and we are driven to aim at something that arises from deep within each of us. That drive leads us away from the need for assumption as we fill in a framework, at least in the area in which we become competent. Nonetheless, limitation is the rule, not the exception. Since knowledge is so profoundly vast, we are left operating to some degree or another on belief and faith more often than we'd care to admit.

The focus on those terms should not be explicitly religious, though if that's your preferred angle, so be it. The focus here is where belief and faith are not optional, because you are a limited human. I believe physicists when they describe gravity, despite my inability to construct an evidence-laden treatise on its validity. I trust my car will start, and if it doesn't I must resort to using COS VAP to forge a new plan, believing that will be effective. If adding gas does not work, I'm forced to return to searching for the faulty component in a complicated system that I know little about. I'm writing this very manuscript believing that there's value to be found in the countless hours I've invested in writing it, even though I can't articulate what that value is exactly. I have faith that the work will be worth the effort.

All of this suggests to me that the nature of faith is that no human can psychologically function without it. If you have faith that everything around will be as you assume it should be, this framework master key also dissuades potential fear that would otherwise take the place of knowledge because as previously mentioned "fear is not conditioned, security is unlearned." This is so your limited brain can consume small bites of the elephant that is the unknown without the distraction of everything else, a sort of castle wall that protects your brain until a value pierces the fortification. Being completely faithless would be similar to being stranded in the wild naked, causing you to be inundated and consequently immobilized by the vast complexity of the reality we inhabit. Some choose the traditional answer which is to have faith in an all-powerful being, originally multiple beings that went through narrative evolution over millennia. Others choose to ignore that faith is an automatic placeholder in their framework that is crucial to functioning on a consistent basis. I believe this component of thought structure is crucial to the foundation of the religious impulse through the mechanism that is described by Jung's collective unconscious.

If the thought structures you create and values you cling to inform your character and skills, then the place where others are building something similar within themselves, where the two beliefs meet, coalesce to create the basis of functioning cooperation and eventually a functional society. If one believes in nothing, then nothing limits their behavior. Consequently, if you have a pattern of behavior resembling a traditional morality, it will be your downfall if you interact with someone who is nihilistic, because they likely won't play by the same set of limits you are playing by. Keep in mind, we all appropriately get upset when someone changes the rules of a game in the middle of playing it. If morality requires other people and exists naturally within us to some degree, despite the fact that organizations surrounding traditional morality may become outdated or corrupt, it's worth keeping in mind that creating your own morality from scratch is nearly impossible. As we aim together at our lofty pursuits, it is the individual who strays that wrecks the endeavor of the many.

# VISION

Few would argue how much visual acuity plays a role in human beings' interpretation of the world they inhabit. We see boundaries and possibilities. We see threats and safety. We see pain and comfort. I choose this phrasing purposefully, because we don't actually see them as physical manifestations on a landscape, for example as you or our ancestors would see a lion on the African plains. The verb *to see* isn't just a result of biology; the language describes a mental attachment outside the physical process. This language describes something our brain is doing as seeing when there is no clear, rational way of pinpointing where that representation exists within the material reality we inhabit.

When I said that we see boundaries without a fence, without a border, or any restraint to speak of, what is meant is that we don't really see anything but what our mind creates. Somehow, we all accept this as perfectly reasonable, almost as if we implicitly accept that the reality of the world and the reality crafted in our brain are exactly equivalent. One might call that conceptualization abstraction, but for our purposes, this merging of realities is that which pays attention through vision.[12] The language we use in describing reality is just the tip of the correlation between sight, cognition, action, and eventually conclusion. Vision is so important that our biological imperatives

---

[12] Bernard J. Baars and Nicole M. Gage. *Cognition, Brain, and Consciousness: Introduction to Cognitive Neuroscience*, ed Bernard J. Baars and Nicole M. Gage, (Elsevier Science, 2010), 175-192.

have struck an evolutionary bargain that allocates around 50 percent of our bodily resources toward the operation of the visual system.[13]

Vision has proven so useful over countless editions of humanity that evolution has given it primacy. Our forward-facing eyes, along with color vision, allow us to focus on a specific point such as a leaf on a forest floor covered in leaves, in contrast with other prey animals that prioritize a less clear, panoramic viewpoint.[14] We are wired to rely heavily on the visual sense over the others, despite those senses having valuable input to provide. To have vision often suggests sight into the future, which alone is self-evidently impossible, without operating in concert with the mind's ability for abstract thought. That importance of vision works as a component in concert with VAP. Absent biological justification, sight has been concretized and disseminated throughout history in symbolic representations as well as contemporary, mythical, or religious narratives throughout the world.

Regardless of the degree to which someone might say the upcoming metaphors or the religious context from which they're derived is objectively true or not, its relevance shouldn't simply be ignored. If a given culture, its access to knowledge, and the words used to morally unite people change within a short span of time such as 100 years, how do we measure the veracity of claims from more than 2000 years ago and beyond? Simply because an accurate claim is reached through different means doesn't turn the conclusion inaccurate. This is an example of how vision informed by cognitive structures creates a viewpoint, which we will return to later.

The bible contends that we should "judge not lest ye be judged" assumedly—by that which is the highest moral value—because judgment is extremely difficult to do accurately.[15] Refraining from judgment of others is met with judging ourselves, first because coming to judgment from a place of omniscience as a faulty creature that is likely guilty of their own sins, if

---

[13] David Atwell and Simon B. Laughlin. "Journal of Cerebral Blood Flow & Metabolism" 21, no. 10 (2001).: 1133–1145. *Journal of Cerebral Blood Flow & Metabolism*,https://journals.sagepub.com/doi/full/10.1097/00004647-200110000-00001. Accessed 7 November 2022.

[14] Changizi, Mark. *The Vision Revolution: How the Latest Research Overturns Everything We Thought We Knew About Human Vision*. BenBella Books, 2010, 96-97

[15] Christian Art Publishers. *KJV Giant Print Full-Size Bible Brown Full Grain Leather*. vol. Mark 7:1, Christian Art Publishers, 1611. *King James Bible Online*, https://www.kingjamesbibleonline.org/Matthew-7-1/. Accessed 26 December 2022.

not the exact same ones, inherently prompts a negative moral reaction to hypocrisy. Religious prompts didn't create that reaction; they are a reminder of how to avoid not being the cause of it.

Judgment itself implies a decision; one based on what we think is right, maybe even moral. There's modern relevance to be found in the story of Adam and Eve. Despite fruit not physically containing knowledge, the representation of humanity becoming aware of morality separates us from the animal kingdom. If I become aware of what can hurt me, then I know what can hurt others, hence knowledge of morality, that is, the fruit of the tree of good and evil. Reactions from predation dangers such as snakes still elicit a powerful and immediate reaction from any human, despite their conditioning to it, from deep within the primordial parts of our brain. Therefore, if I know a snake creates fear or can even kill others, I can use that knowledge against them.

Other animals are not aware of morality, after all, a lion does not consider the morality of hunting a zebra, nor does he use a snake to harm his fellow lion. This self-awareness in humans certainly presents a distinct difference between the mental structures of us and our relatives. The relevance of this concept to modern life reveals that our society does very little to grapple with morality. Our moral deficits are replaced with uninhibited consumerism, predatory capitalism, and self-interested individuals, creating a veritable fear factory where the purported keys to remove the chains are consumer products, money, or a perfect social media life, camouflaging that these are chains themselves.

Even though vision is so crucial to us, relying on sight alone presents an imbalance. If we assume that what we see is all there is to know, or that the way you see is the only way everyone sees, we remove the part of life that keeps us engaged toward fostering what is new, different, or updated. If you are only looking from one place, the rest of the space is filled with assumptions. When assumptions take up most of what you see, contrary notions become dangerous to the whole construct. What we think of as an irreconcilably different aspect of another person can readily translate to what is in the general category of worth being feared.

If you recall, we established that fear is the nascent state of a mind that is only temporarily hidden with new information, not seeking out the humanity of the other begins movement toward the steep slope of fear. When you aren't looking for new information, you are ignoring what language suggests is important: to have vision is to look behind, around, and ahead. When you believe you see all pertinent information, you will never consider that there may be new information to look for. Ignoring aspects of vision such as this leads to fear of the other, and in-group, out-group tribalism is sure to follow.

Whether Adam and Eve were real historical figures or not, the metaphor embedded within their story is worth examining with care. Ignoring such information, in our archery metaphor, is like shooting five arrows at once, with your eyes closed, at an entire group of people, claiming you can miss them all and simultaneously strike their outlines. None of us are that good at shooting a bow. Life is so beautifully complex that you are incapable of seeing almost everything there is to see and therefore everything there is to know. Balance comes with keeping the benefits and pitfalls of vision close at hand, chief among them is viewpoint..

# VIEWPOINT

A viewpoint is the location from which you are looking that defines not only where you are but where you are looking to go, as well as allowing you to see where you've been. The point from which you view encompasses vision, but simultaneously ties it to the restriction of being at a single point, place, and time. It's often thought of as something like a panoramic picture from atop a mountain. The brain allows your viewpoint to be transposed within a mentally created abstraction that can be seen in two general ways. This nuanced duality is the starting point of thought interacting with the world and, though numerous, these dualities are always interacting, a categorical archetype if you will. These dualities enshrine meaning that is composed of different components that are, among other things, competing and inter-dependent opposites whose interactions, aspects, and tendencies are always in tension with one another.

Some of the easiest-recognized abstractions such as this are two metaphors under the category of intertwined duality, the Taoist symbol for Yin and Yang. The married paisleys, having a small amount of each other within, represent order and chaos, the symbolic masculine and feminine, death and life. Death and life are so interlocked that we cannot have one without the other; as a Buddhist would say, "there is no death without life and no life without death."[16] Every day our lives weave in and out of this and other dualities as we are presented with new circumstances and information. Artfully displaying a human constant where what balance there is to be found is in remembering a little piece of our greatest tragedy is the seed of our greatest triumphs.

An important side of viewpoint's nuanced duality, which I'll expand upon in more detail as this text progresses, involves a view one holds about a circumstance or thought they perceive has a positive association. The other side of that dichotomy is what, after integrating the importance of attention, you may be able to recognize and avoid when appropriate: negative circumstances or thinking. This conception of viewpoint operates in concert with attention and perception to help propel action that may result in some benefit for you by capitalizing on an appropriate position from which you are able to see. The acronym VAP—viewpoint, attention, and perception—is used to help provide easy access to these aspects that are foundational to thinking. Concerning viewpoint, shifting the attentive vision of what you believe is positive or negative allows for the same 360-degree view that can be seen from a misty mountaintop. If the duality and VAP are appropriate, the aim will be true, allowing your thoughts and actions to be accurate, just as an arrow does on its path to find the mark.

The second aspect within this viewpoint duality is what is detrimental—detritus or small pieces in the mental space—to achieving the first; it's an arrow that has a hidden crack along the shaft, ensuring upon release its explosive disintegration into countless pieces. Mark Nepo aptly describes one pitfall that exemplifies this when he said, "The mind is a spider that, if allowed, will tangle everything and then blame the things it clings to for the web it wants to be free of."[17] You can be sure that, unless you investigate and utilize a thought structure such as COS and VAP as an *a priori* filter—something integrated before experience—you will create a cloud and blame the cloud for you not being able to see through it. The wisdom Nepo echoes is what occurs when the viewpoint is imprecisely, incorrectly, or falsely cali-

---

[16] Thich Nhat Hanh, *No Death, No Fear: Comforting Wisdom for Life* (Penguin Publishing Group, 2003), 1-24.

[17] Mark Nepo, *The Book of Awakening: Having the Life You Want by Being Present to the Life You Have*, vol. p. 95 (Red Wheel Weiser, 2000), 97.

brated, causing failures despite whatever amount of attention is applied. Beware thinking that is only concerned with one duality, as there is always more to see from the mountaintop.

The tricky part is recognizing when the negative aspect of a viewpoint expresses itself. We tend to react more sharply, simply because we humans are more attuned to negative emotion, even when it may have in fact achieved a positive result.[18] In fact, studies in conditioned attention theory show that if we experience something repeatedly without positive reinforcement, our attention diminishes.[19] Time often plays a role in highlighting this long after we've spent years considering something negatively. Metaphorically, this is when multiple times you've drawn and released an arrow that had a hidden crack; your viewpoint that repeated failures were because archery itself is negative eventually may convince you to put down the bow for good. After one last shot, the arrow fragments. The temporary discomfort you experience from a small shard that may have pierced the skin on your arm releases your minds' frustrations upon everyone and everything within earshot, including that which you're striving to be most like, such as the highest version of yourself, something that is closer to God. When we curse God, metaphorically it is the best version of ourselves we are damning to a hell we create.

What is outside of your immediate surroundings, lurking in the distant shadows splayed coldly many undulating mountains and misty valleys away, lies information the viewpoint may have missed due to the fact that one viewpoint can only see a small picture. What if, as you released your arrow, you'd focused firmly on your form until the precise moment before softening your grip on the string to release when a young child, too incautious to know better, stepped into the trajectory of your projectile? What if the relationship you so desperately sought with all your heart for countless hours, decades later revealed itself as fortuitous for having not been pursued? What if the most profound parts of your life blossomed only because you allowed a dream to die? Appearances can be deceiving. Desire achieved doesn't always

---

[18] R. F. Baumeister et al. "Bad is Stonger than Good." *Baumeister Review of General Psychology* 5, no. 4 (2001): 323-370. *Negative Salience in Memory,*http://www.wisebrain.org/papers/NegSalienceinMem.pdf. Accessed 27 December 2022.

[19] Robert E. Lubow, *Latent inhibition and conditioned attention theory* (Cambridge University Press, 1989), 57-70.

mean net benefit has been gained. A shortsighted shot makes the arrow land short. A singular viewpoint hides things in the mysterious unknown.

A trip to a mountaintop can provide us with a profound sense of wonder and interest, erecting peace in an increasingly hectic modern mind, if only briefly. This is often described as a vantage point, short for advantage, which implies something above and beyond is to be gained from being here. What if you truly believed, as a Buddhist would, that without death there can be no life and without life there can be no death? What if the right viewpoint was the difference between a life you loved and one you resented? How high is that mountain you want to climb? Are you clearing stones or placing them? Spend some time, as often as you can, thinking about where you want to go and what sparkles in your daily life. Maybe you will find a place where a negative conception has covered a space of wonder and awe.

The eye at the top of the pyramid on U.S. currency symbolically represents that, to see from the highest viewpoint, where the most things can be broadly seen, should be elevated to the top of what should be held as sacred by human beings. The concept is universally disseminated, biologically predicated, culturally reinforced, and linguistically echoed. Vantage points should be elevated as sacred because we are designed to utilize them through vision, fundamental to the interconnected nature of our VAP.

It only makes sense that metaphorical representations would align with biology, because we are biological creatures making representations in our mind that speak them to one another, generation after generation. Whether you believe in a divine source or not is irrelevant in your need to utilize passed-down representations to minimize you and your offspring's own challenges. Experience may be the best teacher, but it's often a malicious tutor.

Consider when we say someone's actions were straight and true, as an archer would say. The actions of archery are not common in modernity, but are so profoundly contextually linked to reality that they supersede time and commonality, directly relating us to themes of honesty, forthrightness, and good character. Language being the vehicle for concept, we can now recognize universal patterns, such as Heaven is seen as up and Hell is down, and rising up is categorically good while falling down is universally bad. Despite a different language or place of birth, our experiences have united with consistent patterns across cultures and over the millennia. Generation after generation of biology meeting nature leading to experience represented through language and symbolic representation. These are more echoes of the aforementioned "inherited patterns of thought" of Carl Jung's collective unconscious. This internal mode of categorizing and representing life experience are, in my view, another root in the tree of the religious impulse as well as the historical connection of religious themes that exist through otherwise historically disconnected populations.

When you utter the phrase "You're going down," we implicitly understand that's negative and that whomever it's been uttered to will not be happy about it. When you say you are feeling down, it echoes a sentiment of what is symbolically down, and here's a wasted hint to the reader who already knows: it's not another day in paradise. A verb such as *to fall* has implicit cross-cultural implications that directly connect to our fear circuits, and in turn are represented in our stories. The religious abstraction of Hell can easily be where you land by simply living, even when you are trying your best to aim toward the celestial heaven and even if you don't call your ultimate goal heaven. If you remain unconvinced of how close to hell humanity can make a reality, investigate human history; the depravity knows few bounds. The arbitrary nature of the world is no excuse for adding to its potential misery by aiming anywhere but the top, toward the place from which you can best see.

# ATTENTION

Anyone who has spent time around another human peer or baby, or even an animal, recognizes the importance of attention, but perhaps not as much as it is due. We strive for attention every day as if it is cultural and interpersonal manna—heavenly bread. Attention and cognition are inextricably linked.[20] Militaries throughout history have utilized attention as a fundamental function that glues together the groups within a hierarchy. Over time, those leading people into battle recognized that achieving victory requires rigorous attention to orders, to detail, to the organized hierarchy of the group and respecting your position within the organization. If you broaden this idea to all human groups, then where we are in the hierarchy of people around us becomes somewhat of a self-evident condition, but if not, Christopher Boehm is one of many who can support the claim.[21] Behind the scenes of our conscious thought is a counter of sorts, managed by neurochemicals in the brain, requiring attention to mediate the positioning.[22] When things get really tough, the wise pay attention.

---

[20] Holly Alliger Ruff and Mary Klevjord Rothbart, *Attention in Early Development: Themes and Variations* (Oxford University Press, 1996), accessed 28 October 2024, 135-162.

[21] Christopher Boehm, *Hierarchy in the Forest: The Evolution of Egalitarian Behavior* (Harvard University Press, 2001), 35-70.

[22] Daniel Redhead and Eleanor A. Power, "Social Hierarchies and Social Networks in Humans." *The Royal Society*, 377, no. 1845 (2022): 1. *Philosophical Transactions of the Royal Society B*, https://royalsocietypublishing.org/doi/10.1098/rstb.2020.0440 Accessed 26 November 2022.

How far back do attention and vision track? Biologically, we can recognize these traits in the development of the iris and the white that surrounds it, called the sclera.[23] The iris color juxtaposed against the white makes it easy to track the movement of what the eyes are paying attention to, and in turn we've learned over time that what someone else is paying attention to can provide information about what they are up to. If I'm playing a game like football and I throw the ball, other players are watching with extreme intent to what my eyes are telling them I'm going to do. My focused attention, commonly referred to as telegraphing, sends a non-verbal message to others to intercept the pass. If you are watching a hero and anti-hero across from one another at a table, where positioned equally between them is one handgun, what everyone is directed to see is the eyes, because that tells us about their intention.

Some behavioral scientists suggest that 55 percent of human communication is non-verbal, meaning attention is significantly tied to how much information we gain from others actions alone.[24] Aspects of this phenomenon vary, but one example may be to consider when something within us feels the lack of attention or when too much is directed toward somewhere on our body other than our face. Animals such as a rabbit and fox pay very close attention to whether the other is around, and especially if the gaze becomes fixated. Slow blinking at a cat often creates a bond with the animal, who is both predator and prey, suggesting it knows despite its limited sense of sight you are not a threat and therefore it doesn't need to pay as much attention to you. The alternative is an innate reaction to constant attention, signaling that a potential threat is looming. By way of extension, paying attention to other people is far more biologically predicated than speech.[25] Despite this, most modern humans on social media assume the written word, not even verbalized and almost always imprecisely expressed, is enough to convey meaning and intention available only in a face-to-face conversation. The

---

[23] Charles .Darwin, *The Expression of the Emotions in Man and Animals* (CreateSpace Independent Publishing Platform, 2012), 66-85.

[24] Albert Mehrabian, *Nonverbal communication* (Aldine-Atherton, 1972), 65-78.

[25] Kate Kenski and Kathleen Hall Jamieson, ed *The Oxford Handbook of Political Communication* (Oxford University Press, 2017), 21-48.

reason people are so affixed to social media? I would argue that it's because we crave and utilize social attention.

While briefly on the subject of social media, it's worth mentioning that its explicit purpose is to maximize attention, without concern over truth, accuracy, or reality. Arguably one of the greatest chess players, Gary Kasparov, was defeated by a computer in 1997. More than twenty years later, we've been developing and employing more sophisticated computer modeling aimed at capturing and keeping your attention to sell it to advertisers. We are facing supercomputers more capable of calculation than the best humans, and those artificial entities are easily aimed at manipulating our behavior without concern for repercussions.

Ever feel like you can't stop scrolling on social media? Like the advertisements shown to you seemed to have read your mind, or maybe listened when devices were off? Ever wonder why conversations almost instantly devolve into arguments, but we keep coming back for more? Given that most of what enables us to communicate effectively is impossible on social media, it is ripe for exploitation. The artificial intelligence (AI) that we feared would bring destruction through cyborgs like the terminator isn't here, but it is capable of being directed to master our psychological weaknesses, with one devastating side effect being worsening the divide between us.

If you think staying off social media will stop this divisive catastrophe, consider that it's not enough to stay off and silent; social media will still affect the entire world that remains on the sites, echoing into all lives, regardless of whether they have a profile on a site such as Facebook or whether they use AI programs. Capitalizing on fear creates a most pernicious propaganda, pushing us farther and farther from shared experience. The farther apart we get, the more alone we feel and, consequently, the more we look to satiate our need for attention, for somewhere to belong, such as a tribe. This causes the computer-generated algorithm to supply you with an echo chamber of your beliefs, furthering the positive feedback loop of division. Attention, especially when weaponized, has profound costs.

Some of the connection we are missing while on the Internet is accompanied by a more traditional feeling that exposes one of the most underrated dangers to a human being: the feeling of being alone. The attention other beings pay toward you involves all of our communicative faculties, including verbal and non-verbal cues. That attention supplies us with a sensation from neurochemicals arising around thoughts of connection, importance, value, compathy, or love.[26]

These feelings are not singularly human; as mentioned before, other animals show reactions to attention. A critical marker of the kinds of behavior a dog is likely to exhibit may be best observed by noticing how much attention it pays toward the being above it in its hierarchy. If no such being exists above it, even if only in the dog's mind, all sorts of unwanted behaviors persist. They pull on the leash when going outside without looking for direction from the top or the alpha because, in their mind, they are the alpha. That paradigm is hardwired into their unconscious. The vision a dog uses to pay attention should look to the top—the alpha—for what to do. In comparison to humans, variance in species applies, but attention subsumes.

The desire to not feel alone, especially to not feel separated from likeminded human compatriots, adds to an attention deficit—not the same as the disorder—our brain keeps track of, directly linked to chemicals such as dopamine that regulate things like anxiety and depression.[27] The need for appropriate attention, the kind that is given and—even better—not expected first, is the kind we relish most and maybe even expect. It's not to say expectations have no place in relationships, but we should carefully monitor what our expectations are doing to the development a relationship makes. If you only expect from others and never invest in others, then being alone will likely recur with frequency. The things you expect as an individual will inevitably conflict with the things another expects of you. If a balanced and mutually reasoned tradeoff doesn't occur, the relationship will fail.

One relevant story that comes to mind is that of fish love. A man approaches another who has a fishing line in the water and a fire raging at his side and asks, "What are you doing?"

The other man replies, "Fishing."

"Why's that?" the first man asks.

---

[26] Matthew D. Lieberman, *Social: Why Our Brains Are Wired to Connect* (Crown, 2014), 140-170.

[27] A. S. Brown and S. Gershon, "Dopamine and Depression." *Journal of Neural Transmissions* 91, no. 2-3 (1993): 75-109. *National Library of Medicine*, https://pubmed.ncbi.nlm.nih.gov/8099801/. Accessed 27 December 2022.

"Because I love fish," is the snappy retort.

"You love fish so much you are willing to trick what you love into shoving a hook through its mouth, drag it from its life-sustaining habitat, bash it in the head, skin it, cook it, and eat it? That's love?[28]"

Someone who doesn't recognize the fisherman's definition of love as pathological is, at best, lying, sociopathic, or worse. The brevity in speech the fisherman exhibits underlies his shortsighted thinking, coupled with what he's not paying attention to, his impressively imprecise language and the framework(s) it has informed. There's a significant likelihood the fisherman thinks his words are not worth scrutinizing. What he is telling himself continues to inform his critically unexamined falsehood between speech and action. Twerski puts the crux beautifully stating, "You don't give to those you love, you love to those whom you give," which outlines the concept of love perfectly.[29] Pay attention to someone's words, but attention given to their actions is more likely to tell you what they are up to. There is very little difference between the words we use and the psychological position the words leave us in.

It's fair to counter that story with recognition that words may have specific meanings or multiple meanings, and maybe the fisherman meant that he had a great passion for the practice of fishing. Though the clear point of the story, in my estimation, is to recognize the direction of what it is you are calling love so that expectation and selfishness isn't driving what you think love is, there is more there to unpack about the nature of the stories we tell ourselves.

The idea that differing definitions should be accounted for highlights a weakness commonly ignored in language. If we don't operate on the same definitions, defined colloquially or within a conversation, language ceases to have a productive function. In the case of the fish love story, using love to define something as self-oriented as ending another life blurs the lines of what meaning is ever to be conveyed from expressing the word love. As we rush forward with our lives, ignoring how impactful the simple changes to things

---

[28] Abraham Twerski, Fish Love from Rabbi Twerski, Posted 21 April 2018. Fish Love from Rabbi Twerski, by Abraham Twerski, YouTube, https://www.youtube.com/watch?v=lKG-3nAUQkY&ab_channel=KosherTube. Accessed 27 December, 2022.

[29] Twerski, *Fish Love from Rabbi Twerski*.

such as how we communicate are, we widen the gap between ourselves and the reality we see, as well as the gap between one another, denying the possibility of positive results. We end up effectively speaking a different language, not realizing that we've done so.

Another consideration worth revisiting when not paying enough attention is one that should be echoed on a cultural loop: talk is cheap, but actions are expensive. When someone shows you they don't care, believe them. When you're in a relationship that is rocky, your words will only play a role in describing how to act in concert with one another. The words either person uses will not always tell you what the real motivation is. Someone might quickly say "I love you" when, if you've paid attention to their actions, what is revealed is they mean something like fish love.

You may have noticed attention is consistently preceded or followed by a conjugation of the verb to pay. This is not an accident. Payment of attention is stated precisely in terms of price because attention comes at a cost. We are always spending the limited capital of our attention, even if we actively choose to do nothing. Time, and the limited amount of it that we all have, is inexorably tied to the amount of attention we have to spend. This payment of a limited resource is exactly why giving attention to someone gives them a sense of being valued. Spend it wisely.

If someone tells you, "I'm an expert archer," you rightfully ask to see the accolades, accomplishments, and, most importantly, see them perform on demand. If what proof that person offers is one plaque for second place because there were only two people in the category of competition, and when shooting a few yards away can't keep a group of arrows within two feet, you're going to clearly see the disjunction between words and actions. Consider that the next time an Internet troll tries to cancel you or someone uses some dogmatic nonsense to signal virtue through some performative display. They have paid no attention to what value is to be found in a person where it really matters, and will be caught up in trying to exert power through speech like a caveman with a club. "Words will never hurt me," says the wise child, some of whom then forget that wisdom with age.

With those considerations in mind, we can begin to further expand on the necessity of aim. In keeping with the theme of relevant historical and mythical context, the metaphors in stories and language are intended to guide us as we interact within our own minds, with the material world, and with each other. It is not outside the realm of possibility to consider, when metaphorically interpreting stories regarding something like a sin, it is meant as failing to aim at becoming the highest possible moral creature you can become, closest to the God whose image and likeness you are made in. Bearing false witness, to lie in the Biblical tradition for example, is a mortal—deadly or very bad—sin. To lie, by way of syllogism, is a mortal wound to your personal development, an injunction that it will not allow you to hit the mark and could prove deadly.

If the injunction is to not lie and knowledge is profound, how do we know what the truth even is? If we are honest with others and ourselves, to what degree can we know all there is to know? The word truth itself can have multiple meanings, literally, scientifically, or metaphorically. Some might interpret the previous statement as a falsehood, while others would present more subheadings. Maybe the truth is to be found in the act of looking for truth honestly? I'm not going to pretend or suggest I know what the whole truth is. However, it's at least possible for me to do my best not to lie rather than speak incautiously. If I use language to describe things that are untrue, it is a lie, albeit one likely committed unconsciously. The lie of omission is in need of being genuinely rectified upon its discovery, just like any other. Not lying is a clear enough target that I can aim at, while knowing the truth is far more difficult than, in most cases, we will ever know.

What if lying was a behavior that hadn't been suggested to you as something that was likely to produce negative results for you by your parents, cultural representations, or a religious tradition? What if it was something you still refuse to work diligently against doing? What if you tried to exercise truth and paid attention to being precise in your speech, trying your best to not lie to yourself or others? Might that cause the arrow to fly, as they say, straight and true? What else might we be missing by ignoring these things echoed from the past?

Considering the amount of energy biology dedicates to your sight, with the result of clarity in only a small spot, attention itself is expensive. Given that reality is orders of magnitude greater than can possibly be comprehended, that expensive attention is also limited, making it even more precious. As what is paid attention to enters the brain, a hidden entity aligns our interpretation, assembling appropriate mental frameworks for the situation. Having been pre-built by the same hidden force through years of practice, they are nested inside of and stacked upon other practiced behaviors and are resurrected for the task. Often covered and connected by belief, missing building blocks, or incomprehensible from having expired, the hidden force makes room for only what's most relevant. Leaving the hidden force to its work and returning to the present experience, this is where our attention tends to stray toward what's happening in the moment or referencing a related memory. Eventually, the result is value judgments on what success or failure the experience you have generated or are perceived to have had. Each time, the hidden force shades the building block of that experience with a valuation when eventually, even as the complete memory fades piece by piece, the value is the last part to diminish.

It's easy to see how the vastness of experience forces your attention to miss almost everything but what it's focused on, but why do even cloudy memories have a positive or negative association that's easily recognizable? Attention must be balanced with the phantom that stamps our experience with value, and it is at this point where focus becomes crucial to COS VAP and, in particular, Perception. Attention is a distinct attribute of our functionality, consisting of the union between the current moment of focused mental aim and the prolonged attention to the practiced form that all humans, including a traditional archer, exercises. When one thing is out of physical or mental alignment, when one stray thought causes diverted attention, when one reflexive jump before releasing an arrow occurs and focus is lost, you can be sure the end result is not what you were hoping to achieve.

# PERCEPTION

Perception is intertwined with vision, but goes beyond mere sight; it's how we interpret what we see, much like looking through a lens. We have multiple lenses, some innate and others shaped by experience, that influence how we perceive and interact with the world. These lenses or filters shape not only what we see but how we act and speak, aligning with our goals. This process is often automatic, happening without conscious recognition. Overlooking this critical aspect of COS VAP can jeopardize our future selves.

Perception enables us to connect our present actions to future possibilities in a way that no other creature on Earth can. Envisioning a future potential through thoughts leads to actions, which in turn may provide updates to our perception—if the results are attended to. This brings us back to the call to pay as close attention as you possibly can, which is by no means a revelatory statement; we all intrinsically know every child pays attention without learning why they need to do it. Attention is a perceptual aid of functionality hardwired into our thinking, a gifted lens. We all are inexorably drawn to pay attention to a child we are near, as if we have a built-in priority to that behavior. Maybe that's the brain reminding us to, at times, be child-like, not strictly a biological imperative to ensure the species survives.

While this chapter focuses on perception, the rest of COS VAP are a natural part of the discussion because perception encompasses and is informed by them. Our frameworks, experiences, and innate values all shape our perception, which in turn prioritizes what we deem important, whether it's what components we pay attention to or the order that we choose a viewpoint to see from. For example if our perception of being child-like is only that of foolishness and impetuous self-interest, we de-value the need to pay attention, openness to experience, lust for life and inquiry, and raw emotional drive that characterizes a child-like frame of mind.

# NARRATIVE AND LINGUISTIC ASPECTS OF PERCEPTION

Ancient stories, for instance, might be perceived as primitive or irrelevant by modern standards. We may use logic to dismiss them, claiming, for example, "There is no God in the sky." While the application of logic itself isn't flawed, the sin lies in dismissing the surrounding ideas altogether. This belief may stem from the assumption that our ancestors were less intelligent than us, when, in reality, they simply saw the world through a different lens—one that requires a close examination of our current viewpoint.

Perception is such a vast and nebulous cloud that functional lenses like COS and VAP can easily become obscured within it. While many claim to think scientifically, this is far from our natural state of perception. Consider that if the scientific method were innately ingrained in our frameworks, it would have developed long before thinkers like Bacon and Descartes formalized it. Instead, we have relied on simplifying lenses that are prone to solidify bias in our perceptions, having both appropriate and inappropriate moments for their application.

This fog of bias, innate biological responses such as fear, and dogmatic viewpoints in perception are not unique to modern humans. Those who crafted ancient myths, like the Egyptians, likely used logic at times, applied it as they saw fit, and believed their perception was rational despite the cloudiness of their worldview. Consider one version of the Egyptian myth of Osiris, his son Horus, and his brother Set. After being torn apart by Set, Osiris's pieces were scattered. In a battle with Set, Horus lost an eye, but after defeating him, he retrieved the eye, which came to symbolize restoration and was represented by the phases of the moon, according to the Encyclopedia Britannica.[30]

To a modern mind, this story might seem absurd: how can a torn-out eye become a powerful amulet or embody the moon itself? Such a perception dismisses the myth's meaning entirely, reducing it to something baffling and pointless. If you've ever viewed ancient stories through this modern lens—taking them literally—you might ask yourself: when was the last time you truly applied the scientific method to your thinking? When did you last consciously filter information through a structure rooted in rational hypotheses, testing, and evaluation, free from bias? If you're like me, you may find that you fall short of this mark, and will benefit from returning to investigate the thought filters COS and VAP.

When grappling with the tension between myth and science, we often default to logic and simplified explanations.[31] Using what he describes as "anchors," Daniel Kahneman explains that this is used as "a mental shortcut…that leads people to rely on simplified, often arbitrary reference points when evaluating complex information." Whether we rely solely on religious frameworks or scientific ones, we often approach debates and discussions with the same kind of belief shortcuts, as though a singular viewpoint can adequately encompass the complexities of the world. The scientific lens absolutely has its utility in some areas, but in others it falls short of allowing helpful information to inform our perception. A rigid, singular viewpoint—dogmatically held—prevents us from deriving meaning. Like refusing to change your viewpoint to see a sunrise or ignoring components and order by thinking two sticks and a string equal a bow, you can't expect a good result without assessing COS VAP.

---

[30] Encyclopedia Britannica, "Eye of Horus | Description & Myth." *Britannica*, 1998, https://www.britannica.com/topic/Eye-of-Horus. Accessed 6 January, 2023.

[31] Daniel Kahneman, *Thinking, Fast and Slow* (Farrar, Straus, and Giroux, 2011), 119-128.

Myth, rather than an empirical lens, is often better understood through a metaphorical lens. Given that those who passed on these stories didn't view the world through the same filter that we use today—another filter or lens— this shift in viewpoint forces a new perception and alters the meaning we derive from their myths. The challenge lies in balancing the timeless elements of human experience with a modern perception that can help us unlock their deeper meanings and apply them to the real world. Otherwise, we risk losing the valuable insights—cheat codes—passed down through generations of human interaction.

Let's return to our exploration of Egyptian mythology and keep it simple. Consider the image of the previously discussed eye atop the pyramid, the symbol found on U.S. currency. In the aforementioned story of Horus, his eye, after being lost and restored, became a symbol of vision and power. The eye atop the pyramid can be viewed as representing how we wander into new territory, unable to see from a viewpoint and, after searching, find our focused sight from the highest vantage point. Revisiting this concept highlights the need to integrate VAP using the metaphor to recognize what humans constantly encounter, guiding us through the unknown into what is often seen as the realm of the gods. In Greek mythology, for example, Mount Olympus is the home of the gods, a place where human and divine traits intermingle—failings and triumphs, skill and incapacity, resentment and empathy, pettiness and humility. We may be like Gods, but can never be them.

The Egyptian myths present archetypal representations of another common duality, hero and anti-hero, which can be found in stories and images through the present day. These common reproductions, century after century, should begin to impart how important it is to consciously integrate narratives into our perceptions. These reproductions are intrinsically tied to the highest version of the human mind, human experience, and thus human being. The tales are shortcuts echoed from the distant past, as if your thousand-year-old father spoke them directly into your ear.

These reflections on perceptions projected from the past into the future illustrate how viewpoint and attention are not just related to sight but are intricately tied to what happens when the individual processes observed information. The component of precise speech informs narrative, which then forms a viewpoint. Perception not only flavors and augments this information but also helps anchor it into memory, forming patterns of thought over time. If the sun obstructs your vision while aiming your bow, a shaded lens may improve your focus. If you don't know how to make sunglasses, you can be grateful that someone else has solved that problem for you. These prepackaged solutions, or experience augmentations, are often available at little to no cost—other than paying attention to where you can benefit from others' work.

Perception, to reiterate, is a constantly maintained structure through which we force our attentive vision, which shades the lens through which we see, forming the viewpoint we are mentally positioned in.[32] This is not unlike a filter in a coffee machine, a cheesecloth through which particles are strained resulting in clean paint, or sifting through a junkyard to find parts for a specific make and model of car. This combination of VAP is the judge of what information we allow to be pertinent and how it will be applied to a given set of COS. VAP is the judge of what discerns relevance, potential emotional valence, importance of the information, and, therefore, what we remember. Understanding our perception is, in my limited judgment, the most important mental task we all have.

That judge often plays into a category of nuanced duality by providing both positive and negative reinforcement in a way that's quite underhanded. Let's say that VAP has helped you craft an ideal, something that could potentially rectify the things that are going poorly. In trying to set a relationship in your life straight by holding yourself accountable to an ideal, you become the judge of your actions when moving toward or away from that ideal. Maybe you decide to be precise in your speech, and criticize your partner only for a specific behavior that occurs repeatedly. For example, they've not picked up their clothes again and you've recognized that saying "You never pick up your clothes" is an imprecise component of your speech that results in their rebuttal of some time they have picked them up, stalling the desired change. You've adjusted your aim toward a positive result in part, but if you continue to berate them with pervasive language like "Never," your inner judge will likely criticize you for missing the mark you set for yourself.

---

[32] Redhead and Power, "Social Hierarchies and Social Networks in Humans," 220-225.

Maybe you've found an expensive car and decide to purchase it, ignoring the steps of having the financial foundation to afford it or adding a component of overtime to do so. When the purchase attempt fails, there are a number of components one can place blame on; the hardest perception to have is obviously you. If you choose external forces that you can't control, action becomes pointless, which increases the likelihood of becoming risk averse in the future. If you aim high you might fail, but if you don't aim at all… well, there's nothing to judge, there's no target to hold yourself accountable to. When we choose not to create an ideal, it's a great way to cheat ourselves out of the little time we have—to unwittingly tell yourself that you can't be held accountable for failure because you didn't make an attempt. Time doesn't care about our personal delusions, and I have the suspicion that your conscience is well aware.

One could easily have chosen to disregard an expedition into the content I'm presenting. That would have been done at the whim of perception. If you are reading this, your perception has aligned with the potential value of ideas that interest you, which exists only because you hope the ideas will bring you to a better form/formation. In consequence, the emotional motivation is turned on, which drives further attention, instantiating a positive feedback loop. Without categorizing from the extraordinary amounts of information what we find valuable, we won't find the attention needed to form an accurate perception.

An error in perception is perhaps the most likely factor to cause someone to miss their mark, which is why much of these writings focus on it. Perception is so profoundly complex that I find myself making a rare suggestion of absolutes: perception is everything. Perception controls components, order, steps, viewpoint, and attention. Imagine that archery isn't your strong suit and you're thinking, *I don't want to do this,* or worse, *I can't do this."* By ignoring what could lead you to the result you desire, or by convincing yourself that you can't succeed, you eliminate any possibility of hitting your target. This isn't a cliché, like "You can do anything." Rather, it's a reminder to avoid mental limitations that prevent you from even trying—much like never drawing the bow back ensures that you'll never hit your mark. In this case, the distinction between *can* and *may* matters because you can't hit what you're not aiming at.

This link between thoughts, words, and action is crucial. If you are convinced you can do something, you acknowledge potential—a latent energy waiting to be unleashed. The word *can* represents function, possibility, and performance. On the other hand, *may* implies something more precise: a potential yet to be realized, but one that remains focused on the ultimate outcome. Understanding this distinction is crucial; it prevents you from arbitrarily limiting yourself while still being honest about your capabilities. If your perception is aligned with reality, like a bow and string drawn in alignment with one another, you position yourself to achieve your aims.

This seemingly simple change in words from *can* to *may*, one I'd have readily dismissed in my youth as having come from an overly picky teacher, lays the foundation upon which we all stand. Language, as well as our ability to record and read, brings to life the dead and their knowledge simultaneously uniting us all toward productive ends and is an undeniable key to human success. Language, imbued with the human experience, is embedded in narrative and is a foundational aspect of perception.

The part I, and many others, have missed is how misinformed or miscalculated language informs perceptions that are like trying to shoot an arrow by choosing anything but a combination of a string and balanced wood. Like choosing an arrow that is too stiff for a weak bow, the smallest of misconceptions can lead to repeated failures. More often, these falsehoods are like trying to fire a pebble from a tomahawk missile tube and thinking that everyone else will believe it's something different than a nuclear bomb. Nonsense, right? Sense is nowhere to be found with such imprecise speech, which often coincides with something the reader will have encountered but often ignores: seeking to be understood and not seeking to understand.

Consider the common perception that school is about what others teach you. When we look at just this viewpoint, all the responsibility of training yourself to be capable, articulate, and accurately perceptive is left in the hands of someone else. The grades you received only matter briefly, the industrial-age school bell comes to a final silence eventually, and then most of your life in that place will echo into your future thoughts alone. The misconceptions formulated will plague only you in your future endeavors.

Continuing with the school metaphor, consider how common it is to feel that they didn't prepare you for life. When someone dismisses the relevance of education with phrases like, "What am I ever going to use geometry for?" and you agree without further thought, you've essentially turned your archery stance toward a wall and begun firing. From there, it's a short step to ask, "What does any of this matter?" Small, seemingly insignificant misconceptions can easily lead you down a path toward nihilism—the belief that because we are insignificant everything is pointless. This is why, as Voltaire wrote in *Candide*, it's vital to "cultivate your garden."[33] The imperative here, much like the word imperial, which signifies dominance, underscores the necessity of lifelong learning. No one is exempt from this responsibility, and it should be the central aim of education and a core individual value. In order to gain the wisdom that comes with learning one must do as a founder of western philosophy, Socrates, was told by the Delphian inscription: "Know thyself."[34]

These suggestions to revisit our perceptions are not a command to cling to the dying vines of past beliefs but rather an invitation to do the necessary work: to dig into the mental soil, examine what has failed to produce, and remove what corrupts the fertility of your mind, to understand the parts of our personality, proximal zones of development, and the tendencies that are just as likely to produce weeds as they are sustenance. The goal is to assess what yield might still be attained, if anything. The garden is the ground from which you draw your biological gifts, cultural direction, and knowledge of the past, tuning them through your VAP to bring forth the fruits of your labor. It is one of many metaphors that, if met with inspiration, needs to become part of your narrative and shade your perception.

As you prepare to shoot your arrow, your eyes trace its length, assessing the path from your hands to the distant target. You center yourself, fully expanding your shoulders and locking your body into alignment with the bow. At this point in archery, focus becomes essential. Your attention fixes

---

[33] Voltaire, *Candide*, 1981 ed., (New York, Bantum Dell, 2003), 113.

[34] Jowett, Benjamin, translator. *Plato: Complete Works*. 2020, 262-263.

on the target, and you release. But when you walk up to the target, you realize that you've missed the mark—you've sinned. Even though everything seemed aligned, the arrow strayed.

The appropriate response is to ask what went wrong. But, much like life, traditional archery has countless variables to consider. To know yourself you must accept your inadequacy, which is quite challenging. The world can feel arbitrary at times, and many factors—just by the nature of being human—are beyond our control. Perhaps you could blame God, if you take a literal view of his existence, or the wind he hypothetically controls. But if you ask yourself honestly, neither of these is something you can control. What benefit is there in focusing on your relationship with the divine or the passing breeze when what matters in the moment is learning how to prevent the error in the first place? Taking ownership of your failures is of paramount importance to finding which parts of COS VAP were lacking.

If you can acknowledge that the first step is to correct yourself—rather than abstractly blaming everything and everyone else for things you may have controlled—you begin to see how incredibly complex it is to achieve something as simple as hitting the mark. This realization helps you maximize your ability to avoid sin, reinforcing the possibility that you may eventually hit the mark. As you improve, you also become better at hitting other targets, despite the inevitable challenges life throws your way. When you accept personal accountability and scrutinize your own actions, you realize it wasn't some external force; you had plucked the bowstring, causing the error that appeared downrange. If you believe you may hit the mark, practice identifying and analyzing COS VAP—in the case of releasing a bow string the component of a clean release having been faulty—makes hitting the mark increasingly likely in the future.

As you aim, searching for what lies ahead waiting to receive your arrow, you start to notice something about your view: Your sight is obscured at the fringes or clouded in the periphery. The specifics of even large objects are indiscernible around what is focused on, blurred by the limitations of your mind's ability to process what your eyes see. Quite simply, there are too many things for your eyes and brain to fully attend to, and your perception highlights the image without you even realizing it. Our ancestors were subject to these same limitations.[35] I bring up our ancestors not only to draw a biological connection but also to suggest that something deeper resides within you—something you inherently know but may not fully understand, let alone be able to articulate. This deeper presence speaks to you in the form of your conscience or muse. Over time, the importance of this ancestral linkage will hopefully reveal itself in your life. Consider the words of Miyamoto Musashi, whose wisdom will resonate more with time spent honing COS VAP: "If you know the way broadly, you will see it in all things."[36] This is why balance is crucial—in scrutinizing your lenses of perception, they will naturally align your mind with the pattern-making instrument that is our brain. Musashi also said, "Too much is no different than not enough."[37] Balance in this context means that when you are capable of discerning patterns over time, you also know how and when to apply them. This revelation is the tuning of your perceptions to the inherent patterns of life.

Balance in COS and VAP is something you can both recognize and feel. This feeling is why, when we watch an Olympic athlete reach the pinnacle of human achievement, we all revel in their glory, basking in the triumph as if it were our own. A highly skilled athlete has invested countless hours practicing components of form and the order to perform them in using tools to gain and recuperate in the right steps, utilizing VAP to form their narrative honestly and recognize when their wisdom is lacking. Such achievements exemplify the balance of COS and VAP, and they resonate with something deeper within us—a collective sense of accomplishment that informs and inspires the individual.

An achievement of such magnitude as an Olympic gold medal echoes what we all strive toward, the pinnacle of functionality and the recognition rewarded with a highly prized natural object that shines in the light. Such a star—not coincidentally as high in the sky as anything can get—set a new mark to hit, created a new judge of ideals, and illustrated that it may be possible for all of us to do better. Why else than being drawn toward the

---

[35] Steven Pinker, *How the mind works* (W.W. Norton, 1999), 61-92.

[36] Miyamoto Musashi, *A Book of Five Rings*, trans Victor Harris (Overlook Press, 1974). *A book of Five Rings by Miyamoto Musashi – Free PDF Ebook*, https://www.holybooks.com/a-book-of-five-rings-by-miyamoto-musashi/. Accessed 6 January 2023, 29.

[37] Musashi, *A Book of Five Rings,* 29.

pinnacle of human achievement would someone cheer more loudly and be more joyous at the sight of a sports team winning than an achievement in their own life they've labored countless hours for? The inner self is inherently oriented toward the highest goal because achieving brings with it more than just personal success, but the possibility of lifting the people around us.

Yet, hidden within the mysterious unknown—the part of the world we can't see when focused on our aim—lies significant risk. Although we're relatively safe from the primordial dangers that haunted our ancestors, we remain vulnerable to the instinctive, reactionary responses hardwired into us. Consider the example of jumping when startled by what looks like a poisonous snake, only to later realize it's just a stick. Frameworks help us differentiate between quick, intuitive judgments and slow, deliberate decision-making.[38] This reaction is a remnant of our ancestors' survival mechanisms, but is another reminder of how our perceptions are still influenced by fear and uncertainty, even in modern life.

Once your mind settles back into the knowledge of safety from the fear of the snake, you might laugh at your reaction to jump—it seems silly in hindsight. But in a moment of potential danger, your brain doesn't give your mind the luxury of rational choice. If you had waited to think it through and it had been a snake, slow deliberation might have got you killed. This is why you're guided by the serenity prayer: to change the things you can, accept the things you can't, and develop the wisdom to know the difference. Wisdom is earned knowledge, which is synonymous with security. These are the shortcuts experience has gifted humanity, which in turn shape our ability to use COS VAP.

We have to be wary of not only the clear and present dangers that threaten us from the fringes but also from what we can't clearly see outside of our attention and point of view. We have to discern credible threats with more than reactionary speed, but also use critical thinking. We have to determine when to do what, such as when to hold the bow and arrow steady and when to release upon finding the mark. We have to use our mind to abstractly consider possibilities, and that ability to assess and relate information is what keeps us from doing things like Wile E. Coyote was famous for. This

---

[38] Kahneman, *Thinking, Fast and Slow*, 19-30.

all leads to evaluation and valuation of what we choose to be priority in the current moment. It's not only immediate dangers that we are aware of that pose a threat, the ultimate threat of death looms even before the moment you become aware of it, the nature of senescence; everything degrades over time.

Due to the nature of chaos lurking around every corner, the possibility of another human's malevolence, the nature of senescence, and the time consumption required to maintain and provide required survival needs, we face that which an omnipotent, omniscient, and omnipresent God lacks: limitation. The same God set Adam and Eve toward working and childrearing respectively because they have become conscious of the connection between chaos, arbitrary threat, limits, and the need to sacrifice for the promise of a better future.[39] Despite limits, the need for discerning what is valuable is ever-present.

These limitations should instill in us a profound appreciation for the present moment, yet they are constantly in tension with our uniquely human capacity to sacrifice immediate gratification for the promise of a better future. Our awareness of both mortality and possibility creates an ongoing challenge: we must master the balance between enjoying the present and preparing for a future that is never fully certain. Knowing when and what to sacrifice can yield profound rewards; however, there is no guarantee that sacrifice will bring about the results we desire.

The biblical story of Cain and Abel serves as a stark reminder of this universal truth. When his offering was rejected, Cain was faced with a choice: accept his failed sacrifice and learn from it, or succumb to resentment. This cautionary tale warns us of the consequences when expectation doesn't meet reality. If we are not mindful, we risk being drawn into bitterness, rather than gaining wisdom from our sacrifices. We must remain alert and aware, recognizing that life moves with profound expediency. Without vigilance, time may pass us by before we even realize what has been missed.

Sacrifice appears in many forms and is praised across myths, religions, and tales of archetypal heroes. The Buddha relinquished a life of comfort, stepping away from his father's efforts to shield him from life's suffering.[40] In

---

[39] Christian Art Publishers, King James Bible Online, Gen 1:3.

[40] Hạnh and Nhat Hanh. *Old Path White Clouds: Walking in the Footsteps of the Buddha.* 35-55.

doing so, he voluntarily accepted the painful realities of human existence. The story of Abraham has an eerily similar trajectory, especially given the distance between the cultures that created the tales.[41] Christ, too, taught his followers to "take up their cross."[42] If he was crucified on a cross with humility and acceptance, how hard are the challenges life asks us to bear? Perhaps near the end of his ordeal when Christ said, "My God, why hast thou forsaken me," he revealed the dual nature of God and man: good and evil, order and chaos, light and dark, weak and strong, sin and grace—all hallmarks of the human experience.[43]

It may well be that thinking in terms of God or Buddha has little or no appeal to the reader. Take instead the example of Viktor Frankl, a Nazi concentration camp survivor. By using the extreme example, as archetypes do, it should be easy to recognize that whether from deity or human, profound suffering speaks to all of us. When we assess our suffering measured against someone who survived Auschwitz, it should provide adjustment to our evaluative structures of perception regarding our current circumstances. Of the many things worth hearing from such a noble human, these seem appropriate: "It did not really matter what we expected from life, but rather what life expected from us. We needed to stop asking about the meaning of life, and instead to think of ourselves as those who were being questioned by life."[44]

All hero myths, past and present, are representations of the development of one who encounters the most dangerous of foes, struggling and ostensibly failing to best the enemy because the hero is unwilling to sacrifice that which he most holds dear; struggling, of course, until he chooses to make the sacrifice. Success is always impossible until the hero chooses to adjust their viewpoint, establishing a new more functional perception that incorporates the broadest view possible. The pursuit by one human who builds character and skills along an arduous journey, encounters a dragon holding treasures such as gold or a fair maiden, narrowly survives, but in the end is forged in the fire and reborn a better version of himself intrinsi-

---

[41] Christian Art Publishers, *King James Bible Online*, Gen 12:1.

[42] Christian Art Publishers, *King James Bible Online*, Matthew 16:24.

[43] Christian Art Publishers, *King James Bible Online*, Mark 15:34.

[44] Viktor E. Frankl, *Man's Search for Meaning*, trans Ilse Lasch, et al. (Beacon Press, 2006), 77.

cally speaks to each and every one of us. These are expressions of COS VAP through narrative.

The hero always goes through successive applications of COS VAP over the course of their story. They, like all of us, possess singular trait(s) that are mysteriously revealed to them. To illustrate COS VAP in a more modern hero story, let's review a few applications in the tale of Harry Potter. Potter uses not just any words to summon mysterious power, but specific, practiced, magical words in order and in conjunction with the component of his unique wand to reveal the treasures the world has to offer him.[45] When that wand is destroyed, Potter takes steps toward possessing the "elder" wand, though made from the elderberry tree the word berry is dropped, leaving allusion to the strength that lies in the wisdom of the past.[46] In *The Prisoner of Azkaban*, Potter learns the Patronus incantation, which requires full attention to his perception of a positive memory that influences the strength of the charm. His viewpoint of ruminating on negative experiences requires adjustment before he can unlock the skill.[47]

In *Harry Potter and the Half Blood Prince,* Potter learns the skill of potion making, where following the strict order of steps and the precise components and amounts are the only way to produce the effective concoction.[48] The mastery of this ability requires careful understanding and manipulation of each step. His viewpoint of his childhood and parents evolves as he attends to the new information he seeks out, often in terrifying places such as when he confronts the Basilisk in *Harry Potter and the Chamber of Secrets*.[49]

To round out this application of COS VAP in the modern hero myth, we turn to *Harry Potter and the Sorcerer's Stone*; the stone itself exemplifies how power corrupts and that humility and modesty are the keys to successfully wielding the immense potential as a responsibility, not a toy.[50] Human experience is reflected in this reframing, highlighting that what we pay atten-

---

[45] J. K. Rowling, *Harry Potter and the Chamber of Secrets* (Arthur A. Levine Books, 1999), 85-86.

[46] J. K. Rowling, *Harry Potter and the Deathly Hallows* (Scholastic Incorporated, 2023), 494.

[47] J. K. Rowling, *Harry Potter and the Prisoner of Azkaban - Slytherin Edition* (Bloomsbury Publishing Plc, 2019), 233-235.

[48] J. K. Rowling, *Harry Potter and the Half-Blood Prince* (Scholastic Incorporated, 2005), 172-175.

[49] J. K. Rowling, *Harry Potter and the Chamber of Secrets* (Arthur A. Levine Books, 1999), 221-223.

[50] J. K. Rowling, *Harry Potter and the Sorcerer's Stone* (National Braille Press, 1999), 213-215.

tion to accumulates, step by step, into who we are and makes the difference between the viewpoints that rationalize benevolent or malevolent behavior. The sorting hat publicly categorizes individuals based on its perception of individual character, which is synonymous with the collected values and frameworks that make up our identity, not just the perception we have of ourselves but the identity others perceive of us.[51] Potter perceived Professor Snape to be a nemesis because of his constant criticisms, until learning that the man was something like a step-father, who knew that coddling would not prepare Potter for the trials he'll face.[52] Each stage of Potter's journey reflects COS VAP and the principles that align hum with functionality.

Consider the principle of sacrifice, specifically sacrifice of letting go of the one thing you've wanted most. That burning desire that, after decades of longing and failure, somehow miraculously comes to be, and your first child is born. Returning to the story of Abraham, the call to the hardest sacrifice is commanded when he is instructed by God to kill his son Isaac.[53] At the last minute the command is presented as having been a test to see whether he would be willing to sacrifice what he least wanted to, metaphorically to the highest possible ideal for a human to strive for, to be Christ-like. It's difficult for a modern person to not have only a visceral, immoral reaction to being asked to sacrifice any human being let alone your son, yet viewed as a representation the value of this willingness to profound sacrifice reflects an unparalleled character trait seen only in the greatest heroes.

The legend of King Arthur's round table represents a pivotal break from the traditional norms of social mobility and authority of the time it was written. Despite being a fictional story, the narrative represents a broad-reaching, cultural-wide, perception-changing narrative nonetheless, similar to the leaps of cultural perception like that of the Magna Carta toward individual freedom or the belief that all humans are created equal in the eyes of God. Unlike the rigid class structure that placed knights at the bottom of the noble classes as "farmworkers of noble birth," Arthur's round table signified a revolutionary principle: that one's place among others should be determined by

---

[51] Rowling, *Harry Potter and the Sorcerer's Stone*, 117-118.

[52] Rowling, *Harry Potter and the Half-Blood Prince*, 677.

[53] Christian Art Publishers, King James Bible Online, Gen 22:2.

character, skill, and the unique qualities an individual brings, rather than strictly by rank or birthright.[54] This step toward egalitarianism was, for its time, a radical shift, representing a challenge to established hierarchy that hinted at the values underlying inalienable human rights. This commonly held modern perception of individual rights, usually linked to the Renaissance, required numerous influences and many manifestations over thousands of years to become culturally accepted.

The unique contributions each person brings to the world and shares voluntarily are, I believe, the point of diversity. The necessary diversity of mind and opinion muddies the water of understanding, further miring the truth. The tale of Arthur's Round Table, much of which is likely fictional except for Arthur himself, represents metaphorical ideals from stories that, without first-hand interpretation, can easily be taken literally or dismissed entirely by modern minds. Yet, the liberties I've taken in retelling these tales are often no more provable or disprovable than the stories themselves. This reveals the subtle arrogance of assuming we have all the answers, or resting on the assumption that our understanding is complete—a trait that lacks the humility of a beginner's mind. My intent here isn't to present these interpretations as definitive but rather as one pathway to considering how perception shapes our grasp of what's possible and even meaning itself.

The Knights of the Round Table, embodiments of chivalrous virtue, faced their own tests of character. Morality, conveyed through story, resonates deeply with us because it taps into our intrinsic fascination with meaning and purpose. Otherwise, these stories wouldn't draw us in. Why else are we captivated by different versions of a recurring sequence of events woven through almost every tale? The moral of the story accompanies the earliest stories we hear as children. But what draws a modern adult to such mythical tales—stories that might be easily dismissed by a scientific or rational mind? Even stories we don't want to hear will be interrupted with *"get to the point,"* meaning that we still are interested in what value may be hidden within. I would argue that narrative is the same link that pulls us toward the figure of the Olympic athlete, the ideal of human potential: the purpose that drives one

---

[54] William Manchester, *A World Lit Only by Fire: the medieval mind and the Renaissance: portrait of an age* (Little, Brown, 1992), 16.

toward a self-defined, ever-shifting mountain of achievement that is bound by experienced reality, biology, language and narrative into the packaged lens of perception.

A final interpretation regarding the legend of Arthur is that of his knights' quest for the Holy Grail—the chalice Christ drank from at his last supper. Each knight chose to enter the part of the forest that seemed darkest and most foreboding.[55] For our purposes, the message is clear: what we seek is often found in the place we least want to look. Sure, the monsters of the world are foreboding, but who doesn't recoil at the thought of confronting the darkest parts of themselves? Only those who refuse to look into the abyss. The true hero's journey plunges us into both the world's darkness and our own. As Carl Jung reminded us, quoting an ancient alchemical dictum: "In filth it will be found."[56]

---

[55] Joseph Campbell et al, *The Power of Myth*, ed Betty S. Flowers (Knopf Doubleday Publishing Group, 1991), 150-160.

[56] Carl Gustav Jung, *Psicologia e alquimia*, trans Maria Luiza Appy, et al. (Vozes, 1994), 207-235.

# THE ROLE OF PERCEPTION IN DECISION MAKING

Let's say, given what's been discussed, that you've sacrificed your time in pursuing the goal of trying your best not to miss the mark, not to sin. You've taken to heart the power of biology and metaphor. You recognize the importance of the interplay between COS and VAP and are trying to use those and other considerations that you value to find balance. You ready a grounded stance with your bow, square your shoulders, draw, and reinforce your bow hand, simultaneously engaging the shoulders. You ignore what you can't see, aim with singular purpose, and release when resting your focus upon the mark with precision and delicacy. The arrow finds the mark.

Finding that your aim in life or shooting an arrow that landed true are singularly exhilarating experiences, ones that ring with the dopaminergic fruits of perseverance, competence, and success. Whether it's an easy target, like going for a walk, or it's an adventure of a lifetime, such as trying to hit the mark of raising well-socialized, capable children, the brain rewards with chemicals that reinforce the behavior, following something like incrementally building your character aligned with the voluntary acceptance of responsibility.[57]

Yet, there is a hidden cost to the peripheral haze. By dedicating yourself to step-by-step ascendancy of one endeavor at the expense of others, you inevitably incur a steep price. This reality is captured in Harry Chapin's song, *Cat's in the Cradle*, where single-minded pursuit overshadows the precious moments that are lost in its wake.[58] The value of our choices must be carefully weighed, for our limitations, whether we acknowledge them or not, will ultimately take their toll. Devoting yourself to a single purpose inherently means you must exclude all others. The same focus that enables you to hit the mark also demands that you overlook everything else, even if only temporarily.

If shooting a bow serves as a simulation of life—both a practice ground and a real test with consequences, much like any game—and if you accept the commonly held wisdom that *it's not whether you win or lose, but how you play the game,* then the lesson from any game becomes about how well you internalize its principles, just like any story. Every game offers a set of experiences that, when incorporated into your mental and social framework, can shape how you interact with people and the world. The goal of games isn't only to win just one, but to instill values like sacrifice, fair play, and reciprocity, allowing you to win at the many varied games life presents. It shows those you've played well with others meaning that you are someone they will want to play with in the future. This preparation teaches us how to thrive in future interactions, playing for the sake of growth rather than singular or immediate outcomes. The dictum of *It's not whether you win or lose…*also teaches us that winning this one game is less important than convincing others that you are someone they want to play with, because without the cooperation of others nothing of the world around you is possible.

The key to practicing well is adopting the aforementioned beginner's mind—a mindset free from pride over accomplishments, dedicated to lifelong learning, and unbound by dogmatic ideologies that constrain our perceptions. This approach allows for the fluid application of COS to any

---

[57] R. E. Passingham, *Cognitive Neuroscience: A Very Short Introduction* (Oxford University Press, 2016), 85-115.

[58] Harry Chapin, "Cats in the Cradle" *Verities and Balderdash* (Elektra, 1 January 1974).

skill and VAP to any idea. Over time, the necessary skills emerge, and with enough practice hitting the mark in archery, for instance, becomes increasingly likely. Observing someone truly skilled at their craft often reveals this harmony: what they do appears effortless, concealing the countless hours they've invested. Watching such skill invites a sense of awe, serving as a quiet invitation to imitate the mastery yourself.

Yet, this focused pursuit brings inherent limits. The ability to focus means that certain skills—becoming a software engineer, nuclear physicist, master gunsmith, or professional athlete—cannot all be attained at once. In fact, what we've thought of as multitasking doesn't exist as we often imagine it; rather, our brain oscillates quickly between tasks, creating the illusion of simultaneous action.[59] This misconception, persisting since long before our modern understanding of the brain, is no less a relic of belief than any archaic explanation for human origins. This is one of the many faulty components of the story we have about ourselves that, stacked on top of another, exposes the foundation our VAP rests upon to weak points primed for collapse.

Even if the limit of a person may be self-evident, you still have to choose, and the choice forces you to place more limits on yourself. What you choose to fill your life with is not up to me or anyone else but you. You must push to divine your own path from the recesses of your innermost being—from the Greek muse—in an attempt to make yourself or self-author your own future. Fortunately, the artifice that encapsulates the current societal and economic structure provides you with some measure of choice, though that structure is not guaranteed to maintain itself and is in dire need of updating. An example of an update may be to stop asking children what they want to be when they grow up and ask what interests them in what they are currently pursuing.

The one thing that remains omnipresent throughout life is the necessity of change.[60] Change requires adaptation, but biology can't change quickly; natural selection takes time. This is certain, unless whatever controls the animal is adaptive. The human mind has this adaptive control, and wield-

---

[59] Holly Alliger Ruff and Mary Klevjord Rothbart. *Attention in Early Development: Themes and Variations* (Oxford University Press, 1996), Accessed 28 October 2024, 50-78.

[60] Pinker, *How the mind works*, 519-547.

ing that requires language, the same language that engages in narrative and creates metaphors that at times impose ethics. This presents us with both the need to use previous stories, but also adapt them to the current situations we encounter.

One of the more stark examples of how powerful the abstractions our minds create to represent and influence reality is mathematics. Contemplating from the ground up, the first step is to question—what is any number but an abstract representation—with the help of increasingly complex representations, like $x$=an unknown number, and consequently a formula such as an equation, that describes, outlines, and creates reality strictly from symbols? Bertrand Russell echoes this when he linked math to other productions of the human mind such as art, stating "The sense of being more than a man, which is the touchstone of the highest elegance . . .is to be found in mathematics as surely as poetry."[61] The insights of the mind need continued adaptation as they encounter new experiences.

Keeping in mind this evolution of thoughts and words into products of human ingenuity, I present the case of malaria. The disease that in 2002 alone infected almost 250 million people has undergone what may be to the reader another familiar linguistic adaptation.[62] Mal-air is the Latin root of *malaria*, meaning bad air, a clear representation of where the causal link to the disease—mosquitoes—most commonly reside, which is swamps and stagnant pools. In the absence of scientific proof at the time, the linguistic and metaphorical adaptations have benefited humanity, which is susceptible to the need for adaptation.

Consider the statement *evolve or die* is represented in the Holy Trinity of Christianity, made up of God the Father, who is simultaneously the Son and the Holy Spirit. As Joseph Campbell discusses, symbols like the Holy Trinity carry archetypal meanings that support cultural values and personal transformation.[63] If ever there was a place to recognize how different people's perceptions can be, this could well be it. A literal lens of this phenomenon would take Olympic-level mental gymnastics to explain rationally or scien-

[61] Bertrand Russell, *Introduction to Mathematical Philosophy* (Dover Publications, 1993), 60.
[62] "Malaria." *World Health Organization (WHO)*, 4 December 2023, https://www.who.int/news-room/fact-sheets/detail/malaria. Accessed 11 November 2024.
[63] Campbell, Joseph, et al. *The Power of Myth*, 99-124.

tifically, which often makes it an easy target for those predisposed to only using a singular viewpoint.

Considering a metaphorical lens, however, brings deeper meaning. God the Father symbolizes the accumulated knowledge of the past—a foundation of nearly limitless wisdom built over generations. Yet, like our ancestors, this knowledge is dead, at least in the sense that it cannot independently address the new challenges that accompany changing environments. Jesus Christ represents the embodiment of the wisdom of adapting, coming to life through symbolic rebirth and transformation, which requires access to redemption. This is evident in the biblical account of young Jesus engaging with the scribes and Pharisees, when he challenges their understanding and demonstrates not only a mastery of past knowledge but also an ability to reframe it for the present. The Holy Spirit is the force that inspires and drives such transformation, breathing new life into what otherwise remains static.

What prevents this transformation? The old guard, the immovable authority, the choice to protect oneself at the cost of others, the closed mind. These viewpoints are as vulnerable as a prey animal caught in the gaze of a skilled predator. Humanity's advantage lies not in physical strength or natural weaponry but in the capacity to create ideas and manifest them far into the future, long after the individual has perished. Like a cat wielding its natural abilities with precision, humans wield their intelligence to create tools that compensate for what we lack biologically. Our genius lies in our mind's power, the ultimate weapon that enables us to shape and master a vast array of tools, from a bow to the heights of our modern achievements. This, along with what's already been presented, are why COS and VAP, carefully utilized, represent a few pages in the manual for being human.

Herein lies the genius of humanity, with the word genie as its root. Like the genie bound within a simple vessel, possessing immense power but constrained by its container, the human mind is both limitless and restricted. Culture binds our potential within rules and expectations, much like the order imposed upon the chaos of pure possibility. Yet, this containment is essential; it is only through this structured duality that the genie—our conscience, muse, or even God, depending on viewpoint—can grant us the wishes of growth and understanding. The journey, then, is to find and liberate our inner genie.

Once you discover the genie within the vessel that is your body, you must be cautious with your wishes. Often, the best wish isn't the one that first comes to mind—just as we often see in the stories about genies. The ability to foresee the consequences of our fantasies is another duality, both a gift and a curse. Like those who recklessly use their genie's power, choosing wishes without fully considering their impact, we may inadvertently bring unintended consequences upon ourselves with the words we tell ourselves. Words, one of humanity's greatest strengths, allow us to articulate our desires. One moral of the genie story is that words must be precise if they are to bring forth a true and meaningful outcome.

Typically, in stories involving a genie, the first two wishes are carelessly uttered, bringing simplistic results and shortsighted solutions to their inevitable conclusion, a failure the genie readily provides. For example, a poorly thought-out wish to have all the gold in the world would put a giant target on your back, to say nothing for the standard wisdom that money doesn't buy happiness. Oh, and then there's the reality that if no one else has gold they won't produce anything and you will get nothing in return for the shiny metal. These first wishes are always about immediate gratification and an attempt at direct happiness. Unfortunately, happiness is a result, not a goal. Success comes because we pursue a goal, not the temporary attainment of happiness once it is reached.

The wish that matters is always purpose driven or meaningful because the pursuit of meaning will bring the temporary condition of happiness, at times. What sustains us comes from bringing to life who we are as individuals. If that's the case, you must find your genie within and carefully ask yourself, what brings you purpose and meaning? Remember Viktor Frankl's words—life is asking you.

We aren't consciously directing every connection in our brain or deliberately altering our thoughts until they arrive in our consciousness. Phenomena like dreams—whether visions during sleep that seem to arise mysteriously or the ideal you are striving toward—come from beyond the boundaries of direct control. The boundaries and routines we build over time to navigate the world often restrict our access to the genius or muse that drove us as children, curbing our creativity and openness toward attending to a pursuit.

Consider how a wise person asks for a wish, or even prays. You think of the wish and begin with a problem you want solved, then you consider what the minimal steps are to bring forth the change, and in doing so begin to re-order your thinking. COS and VAP are then the places to ruminate on, where, together with the mysterious dreams, you may come to divine what's valuable to you. This is where the genie may grant a wish to you from the unknown and its unrestricted power, revealing something from within to guide you that sparks the feeling of child-like awe and wonder, an epiphany.

My insistence is that the methodology of our individual mind is worth examining, which takes no small amount of knowing yourself. Knowing what comes naturally to you, how to access the things outside of your wheelhouse, and what brings a spark from within will help you choose your path. In order to choose, you must believe that a given action is valuable and appropriate, from your viewpoint. Belief, then, is both one of the components of our frameworks but also a key to making decisions. This belief is that the viewpoint and its framework(s) being put forward are appropriate. Perception of the framework is what chooses to move forward or re-evaluate. "Everyone believes, from emptiness to everything...and we're not going quietly."[64]

Understanding the workings of your mind is a demanding journey that requires self-knowledge and reflection, especially over time. If the perception that brings you information is not carefully maintained, you are starting with low-quality material, before you even begin to work. You have to play to win the set of all games, and work diligently at the things you know you could improve. You have to utilize your gifts, both biological and metaphorical, to hone your VAP. When asked, "What can one man do in a vast ocean?" the response your conscience should inherently agree with is "What is an ocean but a multitude of drops?"

When your conscience, muse, or passion is informing you, you must be careful not to confuse internal direction with presupposed beliefs. For example, your developed conscience prevents you from throwing a tantrum

---

[64] John Mayer, "Belief." *Continuum* (Aware and Columbia Records, 12 September 2006).

when in the midst of losing a game, despite your feelings in the moment telling you otherwise. If you have ignored the feeling that appropriately directs your emotions to make you ashamed after the tantrum, who you could be will remain hidden. You must embody the hero and follow your conscience back out of the dark recesses of shame that grip you. Prepossession would have you resting on your laurels rather than owning up to your mistake, refusing to investigate your COS VAP, ensuring you will stay where you are until you do.

If you manage to find the courage to listen to your conscience, facing your fear and doubt, you will return after the tantrum with your head low, non-verbally signaling you are aware you've sinned. Every decent parent consistently echoes an intent to provide this lesson through a simplified means when they say, in a musical way, pick yourself up, try again. We could stand to add a part that echoes the need to look closely at why we failed, especially when the child is capable of understanding such things. Something like, pick yourself up, why'd you fail, try again. This may be a simple attempt at updating a structure of immense proportions, but then again, what informed the conclusion of individual rights but a multitude of drops?

Looking at that metaphorical ocean more broadly, we see that culture drives us forward, both narrowing possibilities and urging choices. This same culture, with all its limitations, also empowers us, providing a platform built on ancestral sacrifices so that we may pursue what our genie has to offer. If you have taken the hero's journey seriously, then you are cultivating your garden, imbuing your life with purpose, and striving for an ideal beyond your own immediate satisfaction. Perhaps, you are aiming at the ultimate ideal.

All of this wisdom of the past culminates in what I'm suggesting is the foundation of careful thinking when it interacts with the world. COS and VAP are among the most useful thought filters that may support our interactions with material things and people. Many of the lessons I've described as having been known or even understood before I described them are nothing more than the steps leading up to a foundation of critical thinking. That foundation is laid when applying this filter: recognizing the parts or components of a given task or situation as well as how the steps are appropriately ordered to achieve the best possible result. A successful result is found when the components, order, and steps are aligned with the careful interplay between viewpoint, attention, and perception. COS VAP. The space between what you know and what will help you move forward is where your responsibility lies.

You have to balance on what you know that's been carefully filtered, on what you don't know because there is more to learn, on how to orient yourself to even have a chance to get what you want, and on what and how to change when you didn't get the result you desired. The summation of these writings is the call to build a system of thought that challenges the reactive and emotion-laden mind when that VAP doesn't suit a pursuit. You have to balance careful thought that challenges an individual toward what benefits you and, as a consequence, society as a whole.

To conclude the manuscript, I leave you with my personal recurve bow shooting COS VAP:

Having put in *order* the following *steps*, I pick up the bow and nock an arrow—some of the essential *components*—I begin by squaring my stance to the target. Breathing deeply, I consider my *perception* of each step and the sequence in which to execute them. I think about my *viewpoint* relative to the target, then seamlessly transition from thought to practiced action as I lock my bow arm—utilizing skeletal alignment, not just muscle—to maintain a solid form while I direct my *attention* to the mark.

Carefully tightening my grip just enough on the string to hold it while pulling back as straight to the bow as possible, mindful of the shoulders expanding, I reinforce the muscles straining in concert with the skeletal structure to help hold the weight at full draw. While the body maintains that positioning and form, the mind begins to focus on more than just the broad target, bearing down on the finest possible mark I can, careful to release only when I feel that attention lands on the best shot I can possibly take.

At once all of the previous practice comes to a single point where—just before release—a thought of reinforcing the bow arm and the structure that supports it through the shot rings in the mind when—just as the feeling of being straight and true to mark arises from within—the string hand alone simply goes limp.

# WORKS CITED

Atwell, David, and Simon B. Laughlin. "An Energy Budget for Signaling in the Grey Matter of the Brain" vol. 21, no. 10, 2001. *Journal of Cerebral Blood Flow & Metabolism,*https://journals.sagepub.com/doi/full/10.1097/00004647-200110000-00001. Accessed 11 July 2022.

Baars, Bernard J., and Nicole M. Gage. *Cognition, Brain, and Consciousness: Introduction to Cognitive Neuroscience.* Edited by Bernard J. Baars and Nicole M. Gage, Elsevier Science, 2010.

Baumeister, R. F., et al. "Bad is Stronger than Good." *Baumeister Review of General Psychology*, vol. 5, no. 4, 2001. https://journals.sagepub.com/doi/10.1037/1089-2680.5.4.323

Boehm, Christopher. *Hierarchy in the Forest: The Evolution of Egalitarian Behavior.* Harvard University Press, 2001.

Britannica, Encyclopedia. "Eye of Horus | Description & Myth." *Britannica*, 1998,https://www.britannica.com/topic/Eye-of-Horus. Accessed 6 January 2023.

Brown, A. S., and S. Gershon. "Dopamine and Depression." *Journal of Neural Transmissions, National Library of Medicine*, vol. 91, no. 2-3, 1993. https://pubmed.ncbi.nlm.nih.gov/8099801/. Accessed 27 December 2022.

Campbell, Joseph, et al. *The Power of Myth*. Edited by Betty S. Flowers, Knopf Doubleday Publishing Group, 1991.

Changizi, Mark. *The Vision Revolution: How the Latest Research Overturns Everything We Thought We Knew About Human Vision*. BenBella Books, 2010.

Chapin, Harry. "Cats in the Cradle." *Verities and Balderdash*. Elektra, 1 January 1974.

Christian Art Publishers. *KJV Giant Print Full-Size Bible Brown Full Grain Leather*. Mark 7:1, Christian Art Publishers, 1611. *King James Bible Online*, https://www.kingjamesbibleonline.org/Matthew-7-1/. Accessed 26 December 2022.

Darwin, Charles. *The Expression of the Emotions in Man and Animals*. CreateSpace Independent Publishing Platform, 2012.

Fernyhough, Charles, and Peter Lloyd, editors. *Lev Vygotsky: Critical Assessments*. Routledge, 1999.

Frankl, Viktor E. *Man's Search for Meaning*. Translated by Ilse Lasch, et al., Beacon Press, 2006.

Glassner, Barry. *The Culture of Fear: Why Americans Are Afraid of the Wrong Things: Crime, Drugs, Minorities, Teen Moms, Killer Kids, Mutant Microbes, Plane Crashes, Road Rage, & So Much More*. Basic Books, 2009.

Hanh, Thich Nhat. *No Death, No Fear: Comforting Wisdom for Life*. Penguin Publishing Group, 2003.

Hegel, Georg Wilhelm Friedrich. *Phenomenology of Spirit*. Edited by John Niemeyer Findlay, translated by Arnold V. Miller, Oxford University Press, 1977.

Jowett, Benjamin, translator. *Plato: Complete Works*. 2020.

Jung, Carl G. *The Red Book: Liber Novus*. Edited by Sonu Shamdasani, translated by Sonu Shamdasani, WW Norton, 2009.

Jung, Carl Gustav. *The Archetypes and the Collective Unconscious.* Translated by Richard Francis Carrington Hull, Routledge, 1991.

Jung, Carl Gustav. *Psicologia e alquimia.* Translated by Maria Luiza Appy, et al., Vozes, 1994.

Jung, Carl Gustav. *Psychology of the Unconscious.* Moffat, Yard and Company, 1916.

Jung, Carl Gustav. *Seminar on Dream Analysis. C.G. Jung (Jung Seminars).* Edited by William McGuire, Princeton University Press, 1984.

Kahneman, Daniel. *Thinking, Fast and Slow.* Farrar, Straus, and Giroux, 2011.

Kenski, Kate, and Kathleen Hall Jamieson, editors. *The Oxford Handbook of Political Communication.* Oxford University Press, 2017.

Lakoff, George, and Mark Johnson. *Metaphors we live by.* University of Chicago Press, 2003.

Lieberman, Matthew D. *Social: Why Our Brains Are Wired to Connect.* Crown, 2014.

Lubow, Robert E. *Latent inhibition and conditioned attention theory.* Cambridge University Press, 1989.

"Malaria." *World Health Organization (WHO)*, 4 December 2023, https://www.who.int/news-room/fact-sheets/detail/malaria. Accessed 11 November 2024.

Manchester, William. *A world lit only by fire: the medieval mind and the Renaissance: Portrait of an age.* Little, Brown, 1992.

Mayer, John. "Belief." *Continuum.* Aware and Columbia Records, 12 September 2006.

Mehrabian, Albert. *Nonverbal communication.* Aldine-Atherton, 1972.

Musashi, Miyamoto. *A Book of Five Rings.* Translated by Victor Harris, Overlook Press, 1974. *A book of Five Rings by Miyamoto Musashi –*

*Free PDF Ebook*, https://www.holybooks.com/a-book-of-five-rings-by-miyamoto-musashi/. Accessed 6 January 2023.

Nepo, Mark. *The Book of Awakening: Having the Life You Want by Being Present to the Life You Have*. Red Wheel Weiser, 2000.

Nhất Hạnh, and Thich Nhat Hanh. *Old Path White Clouds: Walking in the Footsteps of the Buddha*. Parallax Press, 1991.

Paine, Thomas. *Common Sense*. Barnes & Noble Books, 1995. *The Project Gutenberg eBook of Common Sense, Thomas Paine*, https://www.gutenberg.org/cache/epub/147/pg147-images.html. Accessed 9 January 2023.

Passingham, R. E. *Cognitive Neuroscience: A Very Short Introduction*. Oxford University Press, 2016.

Peterson, Jordan B. *Maps of Meaning: The Architecture of Belief*. Routledge, 1999.

Peterson, Jordan B. *12 Rules for Life: An Antidote to Chaos*. Edited by Norman Doidge, Random House Canada, 2018.

Piaget, Jean, and Barbel Inhelder. *The Psychology Of The Child*. Translated by Helen Weaver, Basic Books, 1969.

Pinker, Steven. *How the mind works*. W.W. Norton, 1999.

Redhead, Daniel, and Eleanor A. Power. "Social Hierarchies and Social Networks in Humans." *The Royal Society*, vol. 377, no. 1845, 2022, p. 1. *Philosophical Transactions of the Royal Society B*, https://royalsocietypublishing.org/doi/10.1098/rstb.2020.0440. Accessed 26 November 2022.

Rowling, J. K. *Harry Potter and the Chamber of Secrets*. Arthur A. Levine Books, 1999.

Rowling, J. K. *Harry Potter and the Deathly Hallows (Harry Potter, Book 7)*. Scholastic Incorporated, 2023.

Rowling, J. K. *Harry Potter and the Half-Blood Prince*. Scholastic Incorporated, 2005.

Rowling, J. K. *Harry Potter and the Prisoner of Azkaban - Slytherin Edition.* Bloomsbury Publishing Plc, 2019.

Rowling, J. K. *Harry Potter and the Sorcerer's Stone.* National Braille Press, 1999.

Ruff, Holly Alliger, and Mary Klevjord Rothbart. *Attention in Early Development: Themes and Variations.* Oxford University Press, 1996. Accessed 28 October 2024.

Russell, Bertrand. *Introduction to Mathematical Philosophy.* Dover Publications, 1993.

Simon, Herbert Alexander. *Models of Thought.* Yale University Press, 1979.

Twerski, Abraham. *Fish Love from Rabbi Twerski.* 21 April 2018. *Fish Love from Rabbi Twerski*, https://www.youtube.com/watch?v=lKG-3nAUQkY&ab_channel=KosherTube. Accessed 27 December 2022. YouTube.

Voltaire. *Candide.* 1981 ed., New York, Bantam Dell, 2003.